Reading to Make a Difference

LESTER L. LAMINACK   KATIE KELLY

Reading to Make a Difference

Using Literature to
Help Students Speak Freely,
Think Deeply, and Take Action

HEINEMANN
Portsmouth, NH

Heinemann

361 Hanover Street

Portsmouth, NH 03801–3912

www.heinemann.com

Offices and agents throughout the world

The authors and publisher wish to thank those who have generously given permission to reprint borrowed material:

Nikki Grimes Facebook post, July 22, 2017. Copyright © 2017 by Nikki Grimes. Used by permission of Curtis Brown, Ltd.

Excerpt from *No More Culturally Irrelevant Teaching* by Mariana Souto-Manning, Carmen Lugo Llerena, Jessica Martell, Abigail Salas Maguire, and Alicia Arce-Boardman. Copyright © 2018 by Mariana Souto-Manning, et al. Published by Heinemann, Portsmouth, NH. All rights reserved.

Library of Congress Cataloging-in-Publication Data
Names: Laminack, Lester L., author. | Stover Kelly, Katie, author.
Title: Reading to make a difference : using literature to help students speak
    freely, think deeply, and take action / Lester L. Laminack and Katie Kelly.
Description: Portsmouth, NH : Heinemann, [2019] | Includes bibliographical
    references.
Identifiers: LCCN 2018050376 | ISBN 9780325098708
Subjects: LCSH: Transformative learning. | Critical pedagogy. | Reflective
    teaching. | Reflective learning. | Reading. | Literature—Study and
    teaching.
Classification: LCC LC1100 .L35 2019 | DDC 370.11/5—dc23
LC record available at https://lccn.loc.gov/2018050376

Acquisitions Editor: Holly Kim Price
Production Editor: Sean Moreau
Cover Designer: Suzanne Heiser
Interior Designer: Shawn Girsberger
Typesetter: Shawn Girsberger
Manufacturing: Steve Bernier

Printed in the United States of America on acid-free paper

23 22 21 20 19 CGB 1 2 3 4 5

This book is dedicated to
those individuals who make a
difference every day by taking
an active stance to question
the world as it is and work
toward more just images of
what it can be.
Thank you for making
this world a kind, caring,
supportive community for our
one human family.

Lester L. Laminack
and Katie Kelly

CONTENTS

ONLINE VIDEOS

READING TO MAKE A DIFFERENCE **ONLINE RESOURCES**
To access the online videos for *Reading to Make a Difference*, either scan this QR code or visit
http://hein.pub/ReadingToMakeADifference-login. Enter your email address and password
(or click "Create New Account" to set up an account). Once you have logged in, enter keycode
SPEAKFREE and click "Register."

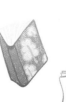

ACKNOWLEDGMENTS

This work has its origins in Katie's ongoing research interests in the area of critical literacy and reading and writing for social justice and in Lester's longstanding work with the power of read-aloud and children's literature to broaden a reader's worldview and deepen the reader's empathy. While it is true that we conceptualized the content and sat at the keyboard and crafted the language, we hope you know that any book is the product of the contributions of many hearts and minds. There are many to whom we owe much gratitude.

We are deeply appreciative of the conversations and collaboration with Lindsay Yearta, of Winthrop University, who helped shape the vision that became this book. We are thankful for our writing partnership that began with #502Writers and has continued with #ThistleHillWriters. These retreats have given us both the uninterrupted time and a dedicated space to think, talk, and write together. In addition, there were many educators who graciously opened their classrooms and allowed us to push into their busy schedules to explore and fine-tune these ideas. We are especially grateful to the following educators for inviting us into their sacred spaces:

As-Sabeel Academy, Greer, South Carolina
Johnna Malici, Principal and Fifth-Grade ELA Teacher

Brook Glenn Elementary, Taylors, South Carolina
Morgan Mason, Fifth Grade

Brushy Creek Elementary, Taylors, South Carolina
Daniel Hoilett, Fourth Grade

Francine Delany New School for Children, Asheville, North Carolina
Buffy Fowler, Operations Coordinator
Elana Froehlich, Title One Teacher
Jennie Robinette, Kindergarten
Britney Ross, First Grade
Jessica Roberts, Second Grade
Roslyn Clapp, Third Grade

Grove Elementary, Piedmont, South Carolina
Marie Havran, Instructional Coach
Jessica Betten, First Grade
Jeanette Montes, Third Grade
Samantha Rochester, Third Grade
Suzie Schmalbeck, Third Grade

Hunt Meadows Elementary, Easley, South Carolina
Sarah McKinney, Kindergarten

Orchard Hill School, Skillman, New Jersey
Eric Slettleland, First Grade

Pine Lake Preparatory, Mooresville, North Carolina
Shelly Sims, Principal
Susan Bukowski, Fifth Grade
Amy Hatcher, Fifth Grade

Roebuck Elementary, Roebuck, South Carolina
Alyssa Cameron, Fourth Grade

Slate Hill Elementary, Worthington, Ohio
Cameron Carter, Second Grade

Southport Middle School, Indianapolis, Indiana
Angela Johnson, Seventh-Grade ELA

Sterling School, Greenville, South Carolina
Dr. Josh Paterson, Principal
Kim Anderson, Third Grade

The Winsor School, Boston, Massachusetts
Lisa Stringfellow, Lower School English Faculty

Wyandot Elementary, Dublin, Ohio
Andrea Phillips, First Grade
Kelley Layel, Third Grade

We are also grateful for Erin Willey for conceptualizing the graphic design of the framework and for the students enrolled in Katie's literacy courses at Furman University for their contributions to suggested literature, annotations, and lesson ideas—with a special thank-you to Furman Advantage Research Fellows Maddie Gonzalez,

Furman University, Class of 2019; Reilly Mahan, Furman University, Class of 2017; and Tatiana Oliviera, Furman University, Class of 2019.

Of course, no book just magically appears from the screens of the authors' laptops to the pages of a book. There are many folks who worked tirelessly behind the scenes to design and produce the book you now hold in your hand. We have come to treasure Holly Kim Price, our editor, as a friend and mentor for her ability to cut to the essence of meaning and bring us to greater clarity for you, the reader. We are most grateful for the skill and dedication of the video production crew, Sherry Day, Michael Grover, Dennis Doyle, Tom Eichler, and Paul Tomasyan, for the great work they did to capture live footage from our partner schools and teachers. Then, of course, there is Sarah Fournier, Shawn Girsberger, Jennifer Greenstein, Suzanne Heiser, Sean Moreau, and Beth Tripp, who have worked their magic to weave it all together into this beautiful book. We are grateful to each of you.

And finally, we are grateful to you, our readers. You are the ones in the classrooms leading students to the deep and powerful insights that empower them to make a difference.

Bridging Understanding of Ourselves and Others

When the reader stands in his own worldview, unable to see or conceive of any other perspective, a book can be a bridge. The right book, at the right time, can span the divide between where the reader stands in this moment and alternate views, new ideas, and options not yet considered. As a bridge, the book enables a reader to span the divide between his current thoughts, views, beliefs, or attitudes and new ideas or insights that may lead to critical thought and new ways of thinking about and living in the world. As with any bridge, we can cross over and never return, or we can move back and forth from one side to the other at will. A bridge enables us to move freely between two perspectives. To cross over does not mean we leave all behind, but it does give us new insights and new ways of thinking, when we return to our point of origin. A bridge gives us the ability to gain new perspectives, the freedom to think for ourselves, and the power to choose what to do with our new insights.

Books as bridges enable the reader to speak freely, think deeply, and take action as a change agent. As bridges, books offer the reader an opportunity to connect to distant places, different views, unique people, and new experiences. In doing so, the reader develops a deeper understanding of himself, of others, and of the world around him.

READING TO MAKE A DIFFERENCE ONLINE RESOURCES
To access the online videos for *Reading to Make a Difference*, either scan this QR code or visit http://hein.pub/ReadingToMakeADifference-login. Enter your email address and password (or click "Create New Account" to set up an account). Once you have logged in, enter keycode SPEAKFREE and click "Register."

Our students are at the heart of our classroom and instructional decisions. Think about each of your students. How do you make their experiences in the classroom comfortable and safe based on your knowledge of them?

Can they see themselves reflected in the literature included in your classroom library?
Do they find characters that look like them? Talk like them? Act like them?
Do they find characters that struggle with similar issues and share similar joys?
Do they meet characters that live in similar neighborhoods or dwellings?
Are the family dynamics in the books similar to their own?
Can they recognize the communities, customs, and lived experiences?

When readers find reflections of themselves in literature, they are more likely to feel both visible and valued and are therefore more engaged in the reading experience. When students have these experiences with literature, Rudine Sims Bishop (1990) refers to those books as mirrors.

Books as Mirrors

The more choices we have the more we are able to be our authentic selves.

—Lesléa Newman

Bella, a first-grade student, became increasingly frustrated when she noticed that most of the female characters in the books she read were princesses or conformed to traditional gender stereotypes such as dancing, playing with dolls, or simply loving the color pink. "Why can't there be more girl characters like me?" Bella wondered. With the help of her family, Bella soon began to discover books that broke gender stereotypes. For instance, Bella connected with books like *Isabella: Girl in Charge* by Jennifer Fosberry; *Rosie Revere, Engineer*, by Andrea Beaty; and *Not Every Princess* by Jeffrey Bone and Lisa Bone, all of which depict females as individuals capable of taking a stand and making changes in the world. These books became mirrors for Bella as she saw characters more like herself who stray from traditional gender roles.

Perhaps our first mirrors, the ones that first influence our identity, are the faces of our caregivers. Our sense of self and our notions of who we are and what is right and just are shaped throughout our lives. Those early mirrors may also include the foods we eat, the music we hear, or the ways we and those around us speak. They show what is valued and cherished, what is undesirable and rejected, and whom we can trust and whom we cannot. Our early mirrors reflect and help form our emerging sense of justice and equity, fairness and equality, responsibility and integrity. These first mirrors establish a child's sense of what is normal within their world. For some children whose identities are not represented by the Eurocentric, heteronormative, cisgender-dominant culture, these mirrors may be absent or limited at school and in the books they find there. This sends a message defining what is important and what is not important at school (Boyd, Causey, and Galda 2015). As educators, we must value all students' voices, concerns, and lived experiences if they are to thrive in our care.

A child's emerging notion of her place in the world may be challenged when she walks down the long corridors of school and crosses the threshold of her first classroom. She may find herself away from the safety net of family and familiar people, sitting among new faces and attempting to make sense of new procedures and freedoms and limits. School may be the place where a child first encounters faces, stories, beliefs, foods, music, rituals, routines, and celebrations that stretch beyond her sense of what is "normal." She may struggle with that idea. She may search for the familiar. She may be challenged by the notion that what she knows as truth is not what she experiences in the classroom. As children leave the known and step into school, they naturally look for the familiar in the new setting.

When a reader is unable to find a reflection of herself in the books in her classroom, the experience sends a message that readers like her are not valued (Bishop 1990; Boyd, Causey, and Galda 2015). According to Bishop, "When the images they see are distorted, negative, or laughable, they learn a powerful lesson about how they are devalued in the society of which they are a part" (1990). Authors Walter Dean Myers (2014) and Nikki Grimes (2016) have shared how books did not reflect their realities growing up. Those childhood experiences led both Myers and Grimes to represent their realities in their own writing to provide mirrors for young readers who have been underrepresented in literature. Children need to be able to see their race, culture, family dynamics, neighborhoods, and experiences, as well as their triumphs and tribulations, represented in books.

As educators, it is our responsibility to draft policy and implement practice that creates an environment where children feel welcome, valued, and respected.

Children are more engaged in reading when their stories are honored and they are able to identify with the characters in the books they read (Au 1980). Engagement in reading is essential and, as John T. Guthrie and Allan Wigfield (2000) point out, it is "strongly associated with reading achievement" (404). A key aspect of engagement is motivation (Guthrie, Wigfield, and You 2012). Without motivation, students fail to engage and develop as effective readers (Gambrell 2011). One way we can motivate students as readers is to include diverse books in our classroom libraries. The use of culturally relevant texts improves motivation and increases students' abilities to make connections and interpret text (Christ and Sharma 2018; Garth-McCullough 2008; Keene and Zimmermann 2007; Tatum and Muhammad 2012).

When we read books with characters similar to ourselves, we envision connections to the world, come to feel secure and valued in our own right, and enhance our sense of belonging and self-affirmation (Botelho and Rudman 2009; Pennell, Wollak, and Koppenhaver 2017). When readers see reflections of similar thoughts, feelings, and experiences, they can begin to envision connections to the world and its possibilities. Therefore, it is equally important for readers to broaden their sense of the world through literature. We want readers to see themselves and other perspectives as they share vicariously in experiences in the texts they read.

Exposure to characters that open the blinds in those windows lets a reader see a bigger, broader world and view a reality beyond what is known through personal experience. It doesn't pressure the reader to abandon her current notions of the world; it merely makes her aware that there is more out there than she knew.

TAKE A MOMENT TO REFLECT

Consider all you know about the students you teach. How does that insight help you select texts that can be windows for them?

Does your classroom library have books that will introduce them to new ways of being?

Will individual students have an opportunity to explore neighborhoods and dwellings unlike their own?

Will they meet characters that have family structures different from what they experience?

Will they experience new religious or cultural traditions and/or celebrations?

Will they meet characters who face new challenges and different obstacles than those they know?

Will they find characters that approach problems in ways they have not considered?

As you reflect on your insights about your students and the books in your classroom library, which topics, settings, characters, and situations are missing? ∎

Books as Windows

When a male student in Daniel Hoilett's second-grade class was reading the book *My Princess Boy* by Cheryl Kilodavis, one of his classmates laughed and proclaimed that book was for girls. Capitalizing on this teachable moment, Daniel read aloud *My Princess Boy* to the class. After reading, they discussed how this book created a window into an identity that defies gender norms. They explored how individuals are often bullied based on appearances. Students shared connections including a boy who is made fun of for dressing fancy at church and a girl at school who dresses like a boy. One student shared that his sister also dresses like a boy but "she can be who she wants to be and that's okay." Using this comment as a springboard, Daniel asked students to consider the author's message of *My Princess Boy*. "Boys and girls can wear whatever they want," one student shared. "Imagine how that kid must feel when people make fun of him about what he is wearing," another added. A boy agreed and said that anyone can read *My Princess Boy* and that people should always stand up for someone who is being bullied because "there's nothing wrong with anyone wearing a dress." Collectively, they decided that the author aimed to show readers that someone will always love them no matter what.

Some texts affirm our lives based on similarities and connections, while others provide us a window into the unfamiliar. Literature as windows allows a reader to stand safely in her own identity while exploring a world beyond her current view. When books serve as windows, readers have the opportunity to consider new ideas and new ways of thinking and to see themselves as part of a larger community.

As seen in the example from Daniel's classroom, literature as windows can also serve as counternarratives, allowing us to contest stereotypes and bias (Boutte 2008). This is vital for children of privileged groups as they explore their place within a larger, more pluralistic world. If the only characters that children are exposed to look like, sound like, and act like them, they are at risk of developing ethnocentric notions of themselves and the world around them as well as notions of otherness that can lead to devaluing anyone who is different. Reading texts with diverse perspectives allows us to explore the multidimensions of humanity and create more inclusive classrooms reflective of our broader society (Boutte 2008). Furthermore, in an uncertain world where inequality pervades society, reading books with characters and settings different from their own can help children build empathy and cultivate compassion, by allowing them to imagine life beyond the one they live. Literature enhances our understanding of one another and promotes respect for other ways of being as we explore how humanity connects us (Kurkjian and Livingston 2007).

As Bishop (1990) has noted, "Literacy transforms human experience and reflects it back to us, and in that reflection we can see our lives and experiences as part of a larger human experience." When books are read as both windows and mirrors, they become sliding glass doors between two worlds celebrating similarities and differences of the common human experience. Sue Mankiw and Janis Strasser (2013) point out that literature provides readers with opportunities to interact with "characters they have yet to meet in real life, but with whom they have much in common" (85).

Books as Doors

After reading the book *A Long Walk to Water* by Linda Sue Park, fifth graders in Lindsay Yearta's class were inspired to learn more about the main character, Salva Dut. Knowing that the novel was based on a true story, one student Googled Salva Dut to learn more about his life. She quickly found his website, Water for South Sudan (www.waterforsouthsudan.org), and began reading about the nonprofit's efforts to build wells to bring clean drinking water to South Sudan. Reading the book *A Long Walk to Water* opened a door for this student as she expanded her interests in learning more about the geography, the issues that affect the area, and ways to help. As she read about Salva's nonprofit, she was energized to organize a fund-raiser. She encouraged her classmates to join her in creating posters to advertise a penny drive at the school. After a couple of weeks, they proudly collected and donated the funds to Water for South Sudan.

Literature can serve as a window to give the reader a different view. That new view can open a door to facilitate action and change. We want readers to explore both the connections between their own worlds and those they read about and how they see themselves and others in new ways as a result. We want them to be moved into action. We want them to move beyond believing that donating money to causes is the only action they can take. The power of literature is that it can build schemata, background knowledge, and vocabulary that enable readers to question why the problems exist in the first place. Those insights scaffold thinking to expand readers' understanding and give them voices to communicate with others to advocate for change.

We believe that children's literature offers a shared experience for all students in a classroom community to consider how ways of being can be a mirror, a window, and ultimately a sliding glass door connecting their lives with the lives of others as they move between worlds. When children see themselves and see others, they can see similarities as well as differences and move beyond a one-dimensional view of themselves and the world. "By offering students positive, diverse experiences that open their minds to new and different worlds," Melissa J. St. Amour (2003) writes, "educators are allowing children the opportunity to expand their own minds within the realm of the classroom and the world at large" (48).

> *Education is the most powerful weapon which you can use to change the world.*
>
> —Nelson Mandela

Getting Started

The responsibility to gather a collection of texts with both breadth and depth sufficient to avoid a one-dimensional view of any topic is challenging. Therefore, we suggest a variety of authentic literature to help readers shape their views of themselves and the world around them (Boyd, Causey, and Galda 2015). Exposing children to authentic literature allows them to experience life through characters that are similar to themselves as well as those that are different from themselves, thus disrupting what Chimamanda Ngozi Adichie (2009) refers to as the "single story." We consider a broad definition of diversity that mirrors society and includes race, ethnicity, religion, gender, sexuality, family structure, social status, homes, language, and abilities.

Recent movements such as the We Need Diverse Books campaign have increased awareness of the need for diverse literature, but it isn't enough. Nikki Grimes reminds us, "Years ago, we talked about the growing need for multicultural books for children. Today, we talk about the need for diversity in children's literature. We're quite adept at altering our semantics, less adept at altering the substance of our actions" (Facebook post, July 23, 2017).

We are aware that you will need to tailor the book selection and direction of the conversations and activities based on the needs, interests, and backgrounds of the students you teach. We suggest you begin by simply getting to know your students. Armed with an understanding of who your students are, where they come from, and what matters to them, you can consider seven dimensions to assess the cultural relevance of text (Sharma and Christ 2017; Tatum 2000):

1. Does the book portray culture accurately without perpetuating stereotypes?
2. Is the book written by and illustrated by someone who shares the culture represented in the book?
3. Does the reader share cultural markers with the characters such as race, ethnicity, or religion?
4. Is the reader the same age and gender as the main character?
5. Does the reader talk in similar ways as the main character?
6. Does the reader live in a place similar to the setting of the book?
7. Does the reader have experiences similar to those in the book?

(Adapted from Sims [1983], Bishop [1990], and Ebe [2010])

Creating Spaces to Speak Freely

In addition to the inclusion of diverse literature in our classroom libraries, we believe that we must create safe spaces where students can engage in critical conversations about topics that arise in literature and in life. We position the read-aloud as a shared experience and a springboard for discussion that builds a community where children feel comfortable to take risks, ask questions, and dig deeper into topics relevant to their lives and the world around them.

The books are the beginning, not the end. Louise M. Rosenblatt's (1995) transactional theory emphasizes the role of dynamic interaction between a reader and text and the unique meaning-making process that results from the reader's prior knowledge, experiences, and understandings. And Mariana Souto-Manning and Jessica Martell (2016) write, "The meaning a child makes of a text is influenced by her identity, culture, experiences, and communities. Reading is influenced by who the child is" (82). As L. S. Vygotsky (1978) reminds us, learning is a social process, and when readers share their meaning with others, they

To create a space inside your classroom that is both physically and emotionally safe for your students, Souto-Manning and her coauthors (2018) suggest we embrace the following commitments:

1. recognize the wealth of knowledge and resources that each family and community has, and help students develop multicultural competence, becoming knowledgeable about and competent in their own culture(s) and at least one other culture
2. make students' histories and identities a central and integral part of the curriculum
3. see and celebrate what students *can* do instead of focusing on their perceived deficits (as defined by society)
4. invite students to name and question injustices in society
5. critically supplement the curriculum, making it not only rigorous, but also more inclusive and culturally relevant. (53)

deepen their understanding and expand their thinking. There is a give and take that leaves each with a more robust understanding than either would have had alone. Reading helps us identify with characters or situations to foster understanding, unity, and empathy. We all have stories. We must create spaces where all stories are valued. Shared stories can serve as common ground, a starting point for reflection and conversation. Once we hear someone's story, we are less likely to judge and more likely to consider kindness.

The power is not in the book itself, but rather in the readers who create meaning or co-construct meaning through dialogue, develop empathy, and are inspired as change agents. Exposing children to diverse literature without guidance can result in few to no benefits (Morgan and York 2009). Because children deepen their understanding of themselves and the world through text, it is our responsibility as educators to not only expose them to authentic literature but also strategically guide conversations that lead to deeper meaning, critical examination of stereotypes, and, ultimately, action for change. Reading is a pathway to civic engagement. As Maria José Botelho and Masha Kabakow Rudman (2009) note, "Literature can become a conduit—a door—to engage children in social practices that function for social justice" (1). Books open doors of possibility for a better world.

The learning that comes from an opportunity to converse, to engage in the give and take of ideas to deepen one's own insights, cannot be overstated. When we read and explore authentic literature, we create spaces in our classrooms where children can question norms, challenge stereotypes, and expand their understanding of the unfamiliar, leading to greater tolerance, acceptance, and equity. To scaffold this learning as children confront a variety of issues, we recommend an implementation model, or framework, to help teachers enrich the read-aloud through robust discussion and extended reading experiences.

Framework

We believe in the power of reading, writing, and conversation to stretch the known and expand the heart and mind toward a more inclusive and empathic way of being. We offer a framework that can both deepen and broaden students' understandings, insights, and empathy for the greater human family and world we all share.

The framework involves five phases: selection, connection, reflection, action, and next steps.

Selection

Here we identify the issue and carefully select texts that will offer students multiple points of entry for gaining insight and evoking reflection.

Here are some questions to consider when you select texts:

■ How will the collection of texts expand students' understanding of the issue?

■ What is the intended goal for reading these texts?

■ How will reading these texts leave readers curious? Inspired? Changed?

■ Will individual students have an opportunity to explore landscapes, neighborhoods, and dwellings unlike their own?

■ Will they meet characters that have family structures different from what they experience?

■ Will they see and hear language and speech patterns that differ from their own?

■ Will they experience new cultural ways of being and lifestyles?

■ Will they meet characters that face new challenges and different obstacles than those they know?

Framework: Selection, Connection, Reflection, Action, Next Steps

Connection

In this phase, we create a scaffold for students to share their connections with a character, situation, issue, or topic. In each selected text, consider the following questions:

- How will students make connections across texts to build their understanding of the issue?
- When students have an opportunity to explore landscapes, neighborhoods, and dwellings unlike their own, how can I help them make connections to their own environment?
- When students meet characters that have experiences or family structures different from their own, how can I draw connections so that these don't seem so different?
- When students are exposed to language and speech patterns that differ from their own, how will I help them find value in all language?
- When students read about new cultural ways of being and lifestyles, how will I connect these to what is familiar to them?
- When students meet characters that face challenges and obstacles different from their own, how will I help them build on what they already know?

Reflection

Here we ask students to pause and revisit texts and segments of texts with an introspective approach. We guide students to reflect on their connections and notice ways they are similar to and different from the character(s) in other related texts. Students reflect on the situation, the setting, and the problem, challenge, or obstacle faced by the character(s) and consider how they would feel in that situation. Based on student connections, we move them toward reflection with these guiding questions:

- Which landscapes, neighborhoods, and homes are you still thinking about? Why?
- Which character or situation are you still thinking about? Why?
- Do any of the characters remind you of yourself? How?
- Which character would you want to have a conversation with? What would it be about?
- Which character or situation puzzles you? How?
- What culture, lifestyle, or situation reminds you of your own life?
- What culture, lifestyle, or situation do you want to know more about? Why?
- What situations or obstacles do you find yourself still thinking about? Why?

Action

Now is the time for students to react individually or collectively in a way that can make a difference. Actions may be pursued individually, such as a student's search for further information on the topic/issue, or they may be collective efforts that involve the class, grade level, school, and/or community. Examples of collaborative efforts include starting clothing or food drives for local shelters, participating in rallies for a number of causes, planting a garden, organizing a card campaign for military personnel away from home, organizing a campaign to encourage neighbors to plant flowers and vegetables that attract honeybees, and partnering with senior citizens to knit or crochet scarves for the homeless. The possibilities are endless because the actions are determined by your students and begin to emerge in the reflection phase of the process. Based on student reflections, we can move them to think about taking action with these guiding questions:

- So what?
- Why does this matter?
- Now that you have read these books, how are you changed?
- In what ways are you inspired to take action?
- What might this action look like?
- What can you do to make a difference in your life? The lives of others? The community? The world?

Next Steps

If we are changed by what we read and the experiences that broaden our worldview, one action does not bring this to closure. We want to cultivate students as thoughtful, caring citizens and lifelong agents of change. We believe this work should be ongoing and organically embedded into the classroom routines, instruction, classroom culture, and lives of students. Therefore, although students may take a specific course of action related to the texts and the themes being explored, this work should not end here.

Based on student action, we can move students to think about next steps with these guiding questions:

- Now that you've taken action, how are you changed? How are others changed?
- Why is taking action important in our lives? The lives of others? The community? The world?

- In what ways are you inspired to continue to take action in your everyday life?
- How will this action lead you toward living a better life?
- How will your action lead others to becoming change agents?

TAKE A MOMENT TO REFLECT

Consider a time you were moved to action. It is almost certain that you have been moved deeply by, or felt tension or confusion from, some experience. It may have been a personal event, something you observed, or something you read. It could have been a movie, the lyrics of a song, a news report, a piece of art that caught your attention, or a conversation you overheard that burrowed into your being. Perhaps that connection was deeply personal. Perhaps it took you to a bit of your past. Or maybe it was an experience that awakened something deep inside you, something you weren't even conscious of. Maybe it shocked you because it was so beyond your own experience that it led you to confusion or new insights. In any case, such an experience lingers with you and surfaces in your thinking at random times and often leads you to an overwhelming need to "do something," to take some action in an attempt to make things better or set things right. Perhaps there is something deep within you that nudges you forward, something that continues to bubble up until you simply *can't* do nothing. Pause here for a moment and think. Reflect on a time when you were moved to action. Feel free to write about that time in the margins. What prompted you? Chances are the first force was some connection with an experience, an individual, or a text (book, poem, essay, movie, song, news article, editorial, etc.). That connection likely triggered an awareness that left you with a feeling that this just wasn't right, that something about this seemed unjust, inequitable, mean-spirited, or just off somehow. It is likely that this notion bounced around in your mind a bit. You may have talked with someone about it. If this experience was prompted by a text, you may have felt compelled to revisit the text with more focus or concentrated attention, alert this time to the bit that triggered the connection. Perhaps as you revisited the text, you paused to think consciously and the text became a window, giving you a new view on the topic.

Or maybe you moved to another text, seeking more information or a different connection to the issue. However you moved forward, it is likely that you continued thinking about the issue even after you left the source text. You may have had thoughts of the issue floating through your

Lester and Katie talk with teachers who have used the implementation framework in their own classrooms.

conscious mind throughout the day. Those thoughts may have prompted conversations with others that left you with even more to think about. So you likely found yourself reflecting on the text(s), your own connections, your conversations, and thoughts shared by others or sparked by the texts until you began to feel that you must do something, you must take some action. That feeling may have led to more conversation or more interaction with additional texts, but it is likely to have eroded the option of knowing and doing nothing. ∎

What You'll Find in This Book

We envision this book as a resource for you to explore literature to help students examine their identities and the lives of others within and beyond the classroom setting. The framework is applicable to any topic and therefore can be applied to issues that arise in your own classroom or community.

We escort you into several classrooms to see the framework in action. We share sample texts, the conversations surrounding them, and the reflection, action, and next steps springing forth as a result.

Selecting relevant texts can be challenging (Tatum 2006). Therefore, we share a collection of inclusive texts gathered around critical issues and moving topics in each chapter. The texts are intended to prompt children to read (or be read to), connect, reflect, and take action as change agents.

Throughout the book, you'll find places where we ask you to take a moment to reflect. Please jot down your thinking in a notebook or in the margins of this book.

After you finish the introduction, we suggest you read Chapter 1: Discovering Our Own Identities as a foundation for the remaining chapters. Then, read whichever chapter is most helpful at the moment. Though it is possible to read the book in the sequence presented, you can move in and out of the chapters as you see fit to meet the needs of your students and the specific nuances of your classroom community.

We recommend you share the text sets in a variety of reading experiences (read-aloud, small group, book clubs, independent reading). We suggest you begin with a whole-class read-aloud followed by a conversation to frame and scaffold thinking in a safe space. You might find it helpful to create an anchor chart as you establish group norms for this classroom ritual. Consider some of the following questions:

- What expectations should we have during whole-class conversations?
- Do we raise hands to speak?

■ What does responding respectfully look and sound like?

■ Should we make eye contact?

■ How can we make space for many voices?

■ Should we be taking notes or taking turns as note takers?

See Figure I–1 for a sample anchor chart.

What We Can Do to Support Conversations	What That Might Sound/Look Like
Use background knowledge.	"Something that I know is . . ."
Make connections.	"This reminds me of a character from another book . . ." "This plot is similar to . . ." "It reminds me of when I . . ."
Listen to and learn from each other.	"So what you think is . . ." "That's interesting. I never thought of it that way . . ."
Take turns.	"I think _____ has something to say."
Ask questions.	"Can you say more about . . . ?" "What do you mean by . . . ?" "What part of the text made you think that?"
Pay attention.	Make eye contact. Take notes. Ask follow-up questions. Look for passages in the text to support what you are saying.

FIGURE I–1 Whole-Class Conversation Anchor Chart

Chapters 1–8 demonstrate the framework in action, with suggested texts organized around eight topics featuring examples from kindergarten through fifth-grade classrooms.

Chapter 1: Discovering Our Own Identities
Chapter 2: Making Unlikely Friends
Chapter 3: Coping with Loss
Chapter 4: Crossing Borders
Chapter 5: Advocating for Change
Chapter 6: Sharing When You Have Little to Give
Chapter 7: Accepting Others
Chapter 8: Lending a Helping Hand

Who We Are

In order to do this work with our students, we believe we must begin with ourselves. We hope this book will serve as a window, a mirror, and a doorway for *you* as you read, reflect, and examine *your own* identity, perspectives, and biases and the role they play in your teaching.

With that in mind, allow us to introduce ourselves and to share why this work matters to us. So here goes. We'll start with Lester:

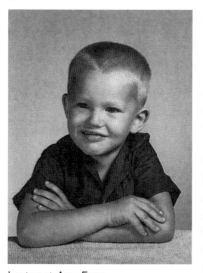

Lester at Age Four

I was born in 1956. Though I was born in Flint, Michigan, I had lived there only two weeks when my parents decided to pack everything and return to family in Alabama with my two-year-old brother and a newborn (me) in tow. Alabama was home to my family on both sides farther back than anyone could remember.

I was a young child living in the Jim Crow South. I lived with segregation. I saw the whites-only and colored drinking fountains on the side of the Tastee-Freez. I attended an all-white school with an all-white faculty and an all-white support staff. I attended church with only white people. I saw people of color, but I didn't know their names or the names of their children. I didn't know what their houses looked like or where their houses were. I knew my house and the house where my ma'am-maw lived, the one where my mother grew up. I knew my granny's house, the one where my father grew up. Those were two different worlds; my house and my ma'am-maw's house had electricity and gas heat, hot water, a TV, and a bathroom. My granny's house didn't have electricity until I was seven. I was eleven before that house had running water and indoor plumbing. The world of my childhood was divided between "town" and "the country."

The worlds of town and country were intertwined, and I moved between them with ease. Almost all the people I knew in town had some relative living out in the country. The worlds of black and white were not as fluid. Although the lines dividing the world between black and white were invisible, they were well established and understood. I knew people who had "help" (a black woman who looked after small children and took care of household chores). Those women came into the homes of the people I knew, but no one I knew went into the homes of black people.

I was in sixth grade when the first black children were allowed to attend the school I attended. That was in 1967, four years after the Civil Rights Act was signed on July 2, 1964, and a full thirteen years after "separate but equal" (segregation) was ruled to be illegal on May 17, 1954. I remember the talk among adults and heard echoes of their sentiments spilling from the mouths of children as well. There was tension, but I was not aware of any violence at either the elementary school or the high school in my little town.

However, the violence was visible in almost daily doses on the evening news. If not daily, at least several times each week there were reports and film of crosses burning, protestors gathered in parks, and the police using German shepherds on taut leashes to push back gatherings of black youth calling for change and equality in cities across the country. TV news brought images of firemen using their high-pressure hoses, not to extinguish threats from out-of-control flames, but rather to force black men, women, and youth off the sidewalks they dared claim the right to walk upon. I saw men covered in white robes and conical hoods hiding their faces gathered to threaten anyone rep-resenting change to the status quo. I saw buses violently rocked and burned by throngs of angry protestors. And one Sunday evening in September I saw a church severely damaged by multiple sticks of dynamite that had been strategi-cally placed near the entrance. Those images came with the somber report of homes, stores, and cars with broken windows blocks away; the blast was that powerful. And this was followed by the news of four young girls near my age who had been killed in that blast. Killed while at church.

All that left me fearful. Not *of* black people, but of those who would go to such extremes in their efforts to keep the world stacked in their favor. This was bubbling up in the world as I was coming through elementary school. The confusion of it, the fear of what you can't understand, is palpable in the mind of a child. It is powerful in the mind of an adult as well. And I was one of the entitled ones: I am white. I am male. Even so, I was mightily afraid. I can't imagine the fears, the stories, the nightmares faced by black children in that time.

As much as I needed windows to the bigger world, I also needed mirrors I could not find. I grew up in the Methodist Church. Almost everyone I knew went to either a Methodist or Baptist church. I knew one family who drove twenty miles to the next town to attend their Catholic church. I knew of a few families who were known as Pentecostal, Holiness, Church of God, or Church of Christ. I did not know anyone who was Jewish. I knew no Muslims. I did not know anyone who was Hindu or Buddhist, and if I knew an atheist, I was not aware of it. I did know people who "just didn't go to church." In short, my world was a Christian-centric, ethnocentric, heteronormative bubble. I grew up in a home with two parents, one brother, and one sister. I knew only a small number of children my age who lived in a single-parent home. At that time, in that place, divorce was still rare and somewhat scandalous. I knew absolutely no one who lived in an open and loving homosexual relationship. In fact, you would have been hard-pressed to find even the suggestion of the existence of a living gay man or woman. There were older women who lived together, but that was presented as an economic necessity for "old maid" women in my time. There were the whispers and raised eyebrows that followed the mention of an older man who lived alone. Most often, the word *odd*, if anything, would be used to describe such a person. Younger boys and adolescents who were anything short of the masculine ideal in the rural South were described as "sissies," and that was anything but a compliment. I was one of those.

I share this here to awaken our minds to the notion that the need for diverse literature is not only about the color of our skin; it is about all the differences that exist within this one dynamic robust human family. It is about finding the roots of humanity and finding how very much we all have in common; it is about discovering the beauty of our souls and the common humanity shared by all who breathe. ■

So now you have a bit of insight about Lester's connections to this project. Let's meet Katie:

WAS BORN AT ST. JOSEPH'S HOSPITAL IN SYRACUSE, NEW YORK, during a severe winter ice storm a few days shy of St. Patrick's Day. My maternal grandparents, Tim and Mary Elizabeth Kelly, were both proud descendants of Irish immigrants. Sadly, my grandfather passed away from bone cancer before I was born. Although I never met him, all stories about my grandfather reveal his kindness, compassion, and commitment to his family. As a young boy and the eldest of his seven siblings, he stepped up as the caretaker when his father left the family home in Brockville, Ontario, in search of gold in the Yukon, never to be heard from again. As a young man, he went on a blind date with a woman named Mary Elizabeth McNamara from Ogdensburg, New York. They eventually married, moved to Syracuse, and had two daughters—Nancy (my mom, born 1938) and Sheila (1940–2017).

Katie's Grandfather, Tim Kelly

My mom raised us as a single parent. My sister, older by nine years, helped carry the load and took care of me and my younger brother. My mom did the best she could with what she had, but we struggled financially. At times, there was no money to pay the bills and the power was shut off. Our car was an old rust bucket plagued with mechanical problems—we were often left stranded in the unforgiving lake-effect snowstorms that are common in the winter months in Upstate New York. We had no savings and no extra cash for maintenance on the car or the house, let alone family vacations or college.

I recall checking out at the grocery store and having to put some items back because we didn't have enough money. This was

Katie and Her Mom

humiliating and I no longer wanted to feel shame because we couldn't afford groceries. At fourteen, I began working and eventually held multiple part-time jobs. I shared some of my earnings to contribute to the household expenses. I saved the rest of my paycheck to buy new clothes. As an awkward teenager striving to find her identity, I desperately wanted to fit in and desired the trendy designer clothes that the "cool" kids were wearing. We disguised our financial circumstances and kept this aspect of our identities hidden so we would be perceived as "normal."

Our family did not have financial wealth and some may have perceived us as broken, dysfunctional, or disadvantaged. But we were rich with love and support for each other. Armed with the strength of my family, I became a resilient, independent, and successful woman.

Yet I grew up in a patriarchal society where I was assigned my father's name at birth and took my husband's name at the altar. Years after my divorce, I completed a doctorate, moved to South Carolina, and began a career in academia. I found myself becoming engrossed in the renewed feminist movement, advocating for equal rights and ultimately feeling empowered to legally change my name. This time I chose my name. A name to honor my truest self. A name to honor my mom and my maternal grandfather. Katie Kelly.

My identity is complex and evolving. It shapes my experiences in the world, which in turn shape my identity. Having the power to choose my name is one of several ways in which I have come to recognize my privilege. As a cisgender white woman, I am also aware of the privilege my skin affords me. Yet as a child growing up in the 1980s, I perceived racism as a horrible part of our county's history. My school was desegregated. Most students of color were bused in from the south side of Syracuse. I was friends with all my classmates, both in and out of school, regardless of the color of their skin. As a young person, I did not think critically about race and the oppression experienced by people of color. I held a color-blind perspective. I was not aware of my white privilege.

I am grateful for those who push me to think critically in new ways and for those who continue to push against the status quo. The more I learn about ways in which some groups experience oppression and injustice, the more I am able to peel back the layers of my own privilege. I am now more conscious of how it manifests in my daily life, from the Band-Aids that match the color of my flesh to the sales associate who is most likely trying to make a sale rather than monitoring me for theft. My only fear when getting pulled over by the police is that I might receive a speeding ticket, not that I might be pulled from my car and be beaten or shot.

I acknowledge that racism, sexism, classism, and other types of discrimination exist. I will not remain silent and hide behind my privilege any longer. I invite you to join me to reject the status quo, advocate for equality, and take action. We must honor all students' identities and their lived experiences. ■

TAKE A MOMENT TO REFLECT

Consider your own complex identity. How does your identity shape you as an individual? As a reader? As a teacher? How does your identity influence the way you live your life? Jot down your thoughts in the margins of this book. ■

Teachers make choices every day. If you only have books in your classroom that feature heterosexual people that is a choice. It is a political choice. You might think this is the norm but you are choosing to perpetuate this as the norm.

—Lesléa Newman

One child, one teacher, one book, and one pen can change the world.

—Malala Yousafzai

CHAPTER 1

Discovering Our Own Identities

When I discover who I am, I'll be free.

—Ralph Ellison, *Invisible Man*

Never be bullied into silence.
Never allow yourself to be made a victim.
Accept no one's definition of your life, but define yourself.

—Harvey Fierstein

In this chapter we take a close look at how identity develops. We attempt to broaden and deepen the definition of identity and the exploration of self through exposure to a set of carefully selected texts that are read aloud, revisited through subsequent read-aloud experiences and independent reading, and discussed in depth during guided conversations and writing opportunities. We believe this topic demonstrates for children how each of us brings a mix of genetics, experiences, thoughts, feelings, attitudes, understandings, biases, beliefs, and family/cultural traditions to the classroom community. At the end of the chapter we provide a list of suggested children's literature that addresses a range of topics such as physical identity, gender identity, racial and ethnic identity, diverse family structures/dynamics, and more. Each selection offers an opportunity to deepen insights about identity and ways we can support members of our one human family.

TAKE A MOMENT TO REFLECT

Imagine an infant.

Hold that image and jot down what your mind conjured. Be honest; no one will see your responses but you.

Clothing type and color: _____

Eye color: _____

Hair color: _____

Gender: _____

Skin tone: _____

Race: _____

Ethnicity: _____

Economic status: _____

Does this infant mirror your identity in any way? Is the infant aware of any markers of identity? At what point does the child begin to think of himself or herself in these ways?

We know a toddler who is sixteen months old and beginning to walk with independence, babble in waves, and have true words in speech. She mimics the sounds of animals when asked, "What does the cow say?" or "What does the dog say?" If you ask her, "Where is Mommy?" or "Where is Daddy?" she searches the room, beams, and points to the parent. She loves her little red piano, her stuffed cuddle friends, and the two dogs in her family; in fact, she loves all dogs. It's not uncommon to find her sitting in the floor of her room holding a favorite book, turning the pages, and babbling some string of sound. Her personality is blossoming, but she does not know whether she is a boy or a girl, black or white or brown, Christian or Buddhist or Muslim or Hindu, liberal or conservative, Republican or Democrat or Libertarian or Socialist or Communist. She does not know whether she is gifted or learning disabled. She does not know whether she is adopted or the biological offspring of her parents. She does not know whether she is gay or straight, cisgender or transgender. She is emerging in the world, as is her identity. Soon enough, the world will begin trying to define her within the parameters of cultural norms. The more important question is "How will she define herself?"

The goal of this reflection is to provide children with literature that validates their existence as real and worthy and beautiful, while at the same time leading them to recognize the existence of others who, though they may be different in some ways, are still very much the same. ■

Voices from the Classroom

The teachers and students featured in this chapter learn together at Francine Delaney New School for Children (FDNSC), a public charter school located in Asheville, North Carolina. The school is a small and close-knit community of learners organized around a clear and visible mission with a stated focus on social justice:

> Francine Delany New School For Children is an inclusive community that is committed to promoting social justice and preserving the inherent worth and human dignity of every person.

As individuals and as a school we will:

- Practice fairness and equality for people of every race, ethnicity, gender, age, sexual orientation, ability, socio-economic status, religious belief, political view and other identities.
- Analyze multiple perspectives on historical and contemporary issues.
- Build a community of critical thinkers who are active in the world.

We are committed to ongoing learning, raising awareness, and fostering dialogue around issues of social justice.

This school community is devoted to developing strong independent thinkers who are kind, civic-minded, caring, and confident. They make a concerted effort to support students in becoming aware of and committing to their best self, both as a student and as a person who is a member of the greater global community.

We join a second-grade teacher and her class to look closely at our physical features—including our eyes and hair, our skin and stature—and notice what features make us visible and known to others. Then we move inward and explore the notion that our identity also includes parts of us that cannot be seen. Through a set of books we lead an exploration of personality and character with attention to behaviors, judgment, attitudes, and beliefs. That leads us to take note of how we are like every other human and yet different and perhaps even unique in other ways.

Selection

Second-grade teacher Jessica Roberts read *Three Hens and a Peacock* by Lester Laminack. This book affords an opportunity for open conversations about the effects of trying to be someone else and the power of simply being true to oneself. In addition, Jessica selected *Skin Again* by bell hooks to spark a conversation about aspects of identity that are inside a person, the attributes that are not visible in a photograph. She then chose *Red: A Crayon's Story* by Michael Hall to take her second graders into a deeper discussion about what happens when the outside doesn't match the inside. Finally, *Sparkle Boy* by Lesléa Newman opened the conversation about societal norms and expectations as they relate to and sometimes conflict with personal identity.

Connection

Jessica opened the study with a conversation about how we define identity. She asked students what identity means.

STUDENT: An identity is what you look like or what you're known as.

STUDENT: It's kind of like your history and your family and who you are.

STUDENT: For example, Spider-Man is a superhero, so he can do awesome stuff. Then he has an identity as Peter Parker, and you think he's two different people.

These second graders' comments reveal an understanding that an individual can have a private identity and a public identity and even a fake identity. Jessica brought the conversation to a close and then set the class up for the read-aloud. She asked them to think about how *Three Hens and a Peacock* explores identity and being who you truly are.

STUDENT: They understand that the other one is actually doing a lot of work and their job is good and they're the perfect ones for their job.

STUDENT: The peacock couldn't even lay one egg, but also it's a male, so it kind of makes sense. Also, they realize that hens aren't meant to be out there being all gussied up and trying to get cars to stop, and a peacock isn't meant to be laying eggs.

As students began to make connections between the theme of the book and the conversation they had about identity, Jessica asked them to revisit the idea of "identity."

STUDENT: Identity basically means who you are.

STUDENT: You need to have a certain identity, and only certain identities can do certain things. That's basically what they learned. Since the peacock has glamorous feathers and it's very rare you'd see it on a farm, so if you were driving by, you'd definitely stop.

> STUDENT: The peacock is like Spider-Man. Spider-Man has superpowers and he has that identity, but then he is also just a person, a regular person. So the peacock could use his feathers to stop those cars. That's like one identity. But it's also just a peacock. That's like another identity.

> STUDENT: They realized that they should just be who they are and do their own jobs.

Jessica brought the conversation to a close and reminded them that she would be reading other books to push their conversation.

Reflection

After reading *Three Hens and a Peacock*, the class continued to talk about identity. Students recognized that identity is more than just what you look like, that there are parts of your identity that cannot be seen in a photograph. Jessica read aloud *Red: A Crayon's Story* to give her students more to think about as they reflected on their new learning. Notice how she gently guides the conversation from details on the page to the broader ideas.

> **JESSICA:** So tell me what was happening with this book.

> STUDENT: He thought he was red, but he was actually blue.

> STUDENT: Everybody thought he was red because he had a red label.

> STUDENT: I think he was blue on the inside . . . but on the outside he was red.

> **JESSICA:** So everybody was thinking something was wrong with him, right? Why aren't you red? It says right here on your label that you are red. But you are not red. His truest self, what was on the inside, was blue.

> STUDENT: It doesn't matter what color you are . . . They were wondering why he was coloring blue, but he was red.

As the students tested out their tentative thinking, the deeper meaning began to bubble up. Notice how as each voice presents a new layer of meaning, others build onto it as they listen, reflect, and extend meaning for the group.

> **JESSICA:** How do you think Red felt when he thought he wasn't living up to his label and felt like he was doing something wrong because he wasn't able to draw red?

> STUDENTS: Sad and frustrated. Worried, like he was broken. Like something was wrong with him. Like no one liked him.

> **JESSICA:** Maybe he felt like there was something wrong with him. But in reality, was something wrong with him?

> STUDENT: No, it's just his label. He was really blue. He just had the wrong label on the outside.

> **JESSICA:** So his label was saying something that he wasn't. His outside didn't match his inside. Think of how that relates to ourselves and who we are. Do our outsides always tell what our truest self is?

> STUDENTS IN UNISON: Nooooo.

Jessica's references such as "outside didn't match his inside" and "our truest self" build off the ideas generated from their conversation about *Three Hens and a Peacock*. Eventually, one student's reflection moved the conversation from the metaphoric (a conversation about a mislabeled crayon) to the literal (a conversation about gender identity).

> STUDENT: Somebody on the outside could look like a girl, but deep inside, they could actually feel like a boy. And that kind of relates to Red; everybody thought he was trying to be red, but he was actually blue on the inside. People can feel differently than what they are on the outside.

> JESSICA: Absolutely. So people can feel differently from what their outsides look like. When your outsides look one way and you feel different on the inside, that can make you feel sad and confused. So what is our job in making sure that everyone is safe to be his or her truest self? What do you think?

> STUDENT: I think that in the book he is feeling blue, get it? Because he was *really* blue.

> STUDENT: I think that he was feeling sad and, like, worried. Worried that something was wrong with him.

> JESSICA: I see the connection you made. If someone is feeling one way on the outside but their truest self isn't matching that on the inside, that can leave them feeling really sad and confused. So what is our job as caring community members for other people? How can we make sure people feel safe to be their truest self?

Notice how again Jessica guided the conversation without taking over. She acknowledged the empathy and the insight while gently bringing the group back to center, back to the individual's responsibility as a member of a caring community. In this way the text and the conversation have the potential to serve as a mirror for any student who sees himself or herself in the plight of the peacock, the hens, or the crayon in these books. At the same time both the text and the conversation are available as windows for students who find no reflection in these stories. And those windows open our minds and hearts to the struggles of others who may need our support and care as they discover their own truest self. (*Reflection* continues on page 10.)

CONSIDERATIONS FOR THE **3–6 Classroom**

Although the classroom featured is second grade, the same books can be used with grades 3–6 to elicit deeper conversations and to teach proficient reading strategies. For instance, when reading the picture book *Red: A Crayon's Story* by Michael Hall with fourth graders, you can explicitly teach students how to synthesize text. Here's a sample teacher think-aloud modeling stop and jots with gradual release of responsibility.

Before reading, say: *Today, we are going to practice synthesizing the book* Red. *Red is a short story about a crayon. Although this book may be about a crayon, I think the story is very relatable. Let me show you how I would begin synthesizing the book* Red. *From the front cover, I can tell that the story is about a crayon. It has a red wrapping around it, but the color looks blue. I wonder why it says he's the color red then? Below are other crayon colors. They all match their wrapping. So we already know something is different about Red than the other crayons. So before going any further, I am going to write down on a sticky note: Before reading, I think this book is about a crayon that is mislabeled red. Let's read on to see what happens.*

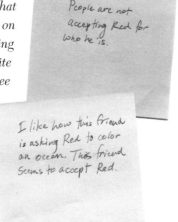

After reading a few pages, say: *At the beginning, we learn that "he wasn't really good" at coloring red. I wonder what will happen? I think he might attempt to color red. I am going to write on my next sticky note, At the beginning, I think that Red is going to try to be able to color red at the end.*

Read on, but close the book after the grandparents try to put him in a red coat. Then say: *Hmm, that's interesting. People in Red's life are trying to make Red color red. They even make him put on clothes that are supposed to bring out the red in him. Here, I am going to write on my sticky note about something I notice while I am reading. I am going to write that people are not accepting Red for who he is. You can write the same thing, or something similar, or something else that you see and think is important to the story.*

Continue reading. Stop after the black page with the scissors. Model writing down what you're thinking simultaneously. Invite students to also write something down. Continue reading. After the page with the new friend, invite students to write down something on their sticky notes. Say: *I like how this friend is asking Red to color an ocean. This friend seems to accept Red.* Read one more page. Ask students to write on another sticky note. Read another two pages. Invite students to write down what they think. Gradually release responsibility by continuing to read but stopping the think-alouds so students do this by themselves.

When you are done reading the story, say: *Now that we have read the story together and jotted our thinking on our sticky notes, turn to your turn and talk partner and tell them what your reactions are to the story. You can refer to the notes you took to help you think of the most important elements of the story.* Let students discuss while you listen in to student conversations. Let one or two groups share.

Provide the following sentence stems on an anchor chart to support students' synthesis of text:

Before reading, I think this book is about . . .

At the beginning . . .

Now I think . . .

After reading, I now know . . .

This is important because . . .

To extend the conversation about identity, we recommend also reading *Introducing Teddy* by Jessica Walton (picture book) with both primary- and intermediate-grade students. To see how these books were used as a text set to explore identity, read the blog post from the Journey Project at https://thejourneyproject.us/2017/06/14/institutional-power-playing-with-fire/.

For intermediate-grade students specifically, we would also suggest *George* by Alex Gino (chapter book). A class discussion along with sample student reflections can be found at the blog post from the Journey Project at https://thejourneyproject.us/2017/06/25/spark-tinder-breeze-conversations-act-of-love/. ■

Reflection *(continued)*

The conversation that followed builds on the connections and reflections from *Three Hens and a Peacock*, ideas from *Red: A Crayon's Story*, and the new read-aloud, *Skin Again*. Notice how Jessica's students got to the heart of this text quickly.

> **JESSICA:** What does the narrator mean when she says, "Skin again is one way small to see me, but not well enough to be all"? [hooks 2004] What does that mean?

> **STUDENT:** I think it's saying that looking at your outside is one way to think you know who they are, but you don't know them until you take time to be their friend. It's like Red because his label was like skin.

> **JESSICA:** So where is the real you? Is it on the outside?

> STUDENT: No, the real you is on the inside. It's in your heart.

> **JESSICA:** It's in your heart. It's what makes you who you are on the inside. It takes more time to get to know someone on the inside, doesn't it? But that's when you get to know the *real* person. Because your skin and how you look on the outside can only tell a little bit . . .

> STUDENT: But it's worth it!

> **JESSICA:** Yes, it is. It is worth it. We are made up of lots of different things, lots of different colors and histories and traditions and patterns that make each of us so very interesting.

It is interesting to note that this set of books moves from farm animals trying to find their place in the community (*Three Hens and a Peacock*) to a mislabeled crayon (*Red: A Crayon's Story*) to a person talking directly to the reader about knowing the real person on the inside (*Skin Again*). Moving through this small set of texts with guided conversation helps children build the understandings they need to examine the metaphoric and move outward toward the personal and human.

To build on these insights, Jessica introduced the fourth book, *Sparkle Boy*. This book presents human characters in a family situation, making the potential connections more personal, making the mirrors and windows more relevant, and opening the doorway to more robust conversations. Before reading the book, Jessica asked the students to examine the cover and quietly think about what they might expect in this story. Then she invited them to share their thinking.

> **JESSICA:** What do you think this will be about? The title is *Sparkle Boy*, so that gives us a little bit of a clue. We can also look at what he is wearing. And if you feel the cover, you'll notice it has texture—it feels like glitter.

STUDENT: I think it's kind of telling that he likes sparkles and that not all boys don't like dresses and stuff. And a lot of boys actually like colors that people say are for girls, but I don't believe that there's colors for boys and girls.

STUDENT: Yeah, some people say pink is for girls, blue is for boys. But that's not true. A lot of boys like pink and purple and a lot of girls like aqua and blue.

JESSICA: We just get to like what we like, right? Whether we are boys or girls or whatever we are, we get to like whatever we like.

STUDENT: There are some colors, um, pink, purple, and things that are glittery, and there are some clothes that I like; dresses, skirts, um, a lot of people call that girl stuff.

STUDENT: One thing I don't like is going to the mall because they have sections for girls' clothes and one section for boys' clothes, and there are girls who like to shop in the boys' clothes and boys who like to shop in the girls' clothes.

Jessica paused a moment, allowing the students to refocus. Then she read the book aloud without stopping. As she reached the end, Jessica invited her students to pull forward the threads of conversations about the three previous books.

JESSICA: How does this relate to our discussions about identity and who we are?

STUDENT: He liked skirts. He loved them. He wanted to be like his big sister.

JESSICA: So, how come Jessie had such a hard time with that?

STUDENT: Because some people think that boys and girls should do different things and wear different colors and different clothes.

STUDENT: All genders can like all different things. Like, girls don't have to just like certain things and boys don't have to like certain things.

STUDENT: So I just want to say that I have a whole drawer full of dresses.

JESSICA: You do, and you enjoy wearing them sometimes because they are comfortable and you like the way you feel in them.

STUDENT: Yeah, when I do, I need to wear shorts.

JESSICA: Yeah, we all do. Whether we're boys or girls, right.

STUDENT: Some teachers say, "Today boys line up first" or "Girls line up first." You could just go first either way.

JESSICA: So we don't do a lot of that in our class. You'll notice that we don't do boys' and girls' things because I don't like to think of you that way; I like to think of you as just little humans. I don't like to divide you up by your gender because that's only part of your identity, but that's not the whole story, right? We are just people and we like what we like. We have preferences and we have dreams and we have things that make us smile and we have feelings. What's important is on the inside. I'm very careful about saying "boys" and "girls." That's why I usually just say "friends" or "students" or "second graders," because I don't want anyone to have to be concerned with feeling that what's on their inside doesn't match what's on their outside. Now, let's return to my question. Why was Jessie so mad and grumpy about her brother wearing the sparkly things, especially out in public?

STUDENT: I kind of think she got mad because when he is in public she was embarrassed. She was worried that people would think a boy shouldn't be in girl clothes.

JESSICA: And that happened, didn't it? It happened at the library, and what did that make Jessie understand?

STUDENT: That it was okay. That everybody can wear what they want.

STUDENT: I think she was mad because at first she was one of those people who think that there is boy stuff and girl stuff. But then she came to where people started making fun of her little brother and she changed her mind.

JESSICA: Because she loves her little brother and she wants to make sure that he feels comfortable and is not teased. That kind of switched it for her, and she was able to see that it was important for him to be able to make his own choices and be able to do what he likes.

A LOOK INTO
THE CLASSROOM

Join a group of first graders in a discussion of identity and acceptance as Lester leads a discussion of the second read of *Sparkle Boy*.

The conversation began to shift and students mentioned how things in public aren't as they should be. There was an extended discussion about the mall and how the marketing of clothing and hair care products is very gender specific. It was clear that these students embraced the notion that identity is more than what we see on the outside. Jessica lifted the conversation and nudged their thinking toward action.

TAKE A MOMENT TO REFLECT

How would you respond if Sparkle Boy entered your classroom? How would you protect that child and create a space for all your students to feel safe? ∎

Action

The best way to find yourself is to lose yourself in the service of others.

—Mahatma Gandhi

A few days had passed when Jessica came back to the discussion and invited her students to spend some time thinking about their own outside and inside identities. These reflections led to inside/outside posters they used to introduce themselves to their peers. You can see two examples in Figures 1–1a and 1–1b. The children in this school loop through the grades as a community, so this class has been together since kindergarten. Though they know each other rather well, these posters reveal some inward feelings and thoughts they may not have shared prior to this exploration. In addition, there may be a disconnect between how one views oneself and how one is viewed by others. Each poster features a self-portrait in the center with the author's outside attributes listed on the right and his or her inside attributes listed on the left.

Taking the initiative to be reflective about one's inward identity can be enlightening. But to share those thoughts publicly can be risky. There is a certain level of vulnerability in sharing your inward self. We felt some of that vulnerability when sharing our personal stories in the introduction of this book. We believe the power here is in the practice of that reflection and laying claim to your feelings and sense of self.

FIGURES 1–1a and 1–1b **Second Graders with Inside/Outside Posters**

Next Steps

To help students consider multiple identities and begin to explore representation of different identities in the books they read, Jessica introduced her students to Marley Dias, the little girl at the forefront of the Black Girl Books campaign. She wanted her students to begin to notice themselves and others in the books they read. They began by brainstorming words related to identity such as *gender*, *race*, and *religion*. Next she showed them a one-minute interview with Marley Dias, and they discussed her campaign to find one thousand books that feature women and girls of color. (See the YouTube video at www.youtube.com/watch?v=OoHBtRhIX-I. For another interview with Marley Dias, visit www.njtvonline.org/news/video/11-year-old-marley-dias-creates-change-through-1000blackgirlbooks-campaign/.) They discussed why it is important to read books with identities similar to and different from their own. Jessica challenged her students to begin to read books through the lens of identity by asking:

- Are most of the characters similar to or different from me?
- Why does this matter?
- How does this affect me as a reader?
- How does this affect me as a person?

(This lesson was adapted from Teaching Tolerance's "Discovering My Identity" [n.d.]. For more information, visit www.tolerance.org/classroom-resources/tolerance-lessons/discovering-my-identity.)

ALTERNATE GRADE EXAMPLE
Kindergarten

Jennie Robinette and her kindergarten students chose to closely examine family identity. Jennie's students come from a variety of family structures, so she chose to read *Lilly's Big Day* by Kevin Henkes, *The Flower Girl Wore Celery* by Meryl G. Gordon, *black is brown is tan* by Arnold Adoff, *Visiting Day* by Jacqueline Woodson, and *I Love Saturdays y domingos* by Alma Flor Ada.

Lilly's Big Day and *The Flower Girl Wore Celery* allow young readers to see a family forming through a wedding ceremony, one heteronormative wedding and one same-sex wedding. *black is brown is tan* introduces us to an interracial family. *Visiting Day* allows us inside another family structure where a young girl and her grandmother prepare for a bus trip to visit the girl's father in prison. And *I Love Saturdays y domingos* invites us to come along as the main character spends Saturdays with her European American grandparents and Sundays with her Mexican American grandparents. Each of these books contributes to the greater understanding of family identity as something deeper and more complex than what the world can see from the outside. Jennie reminded her students of previous conversations in which they explored the notion that each of us has an inside identity and an outside identity. To help her students consider family identity, she suggested that families also have an outside identity and an inside identity.

FOR YOUR CLASSROOM
Consider Titles That Feature Diverse Families

It is important to feature a variety of family structures, including (but not limited to) single parents, stepparents, foster parents, same-sex parents, grandparents as primary caregivers, adopted children, or homeless families. Some additional titles that feature diverse families you may want to consider for your classroom include

- *A Chair for My Mother* by Vera B. Williams
- *And Tango Makes Three* by Justin Richardson and Peter Parnell
- *Counting by 7s* by Holly Goldberg Sloan (chapter book)
- *Fly Away Home* by Eve Bunting
- *Heather Has Two Mommies* by Lesléa Newman
- *In Our Mothers' House* by Patricia Polacco
- *Jin Woo* by Eve Bunting
- *Last Stop on Market Street* by Matt de la Peña
- *Maddi's Fridge* by Lois Brandt
- *The Memory String* by Eve Bunting
- *My Man Blue* by Nikki Grimes
- *The Red Blanket* by Eliza Thomas
- *A Shelter in Our Car* by Monica Gunning
- *Tell Me Again About the Night I Was Born* by Jamie Lee Curtis
- *Those Shoes* by Maribeth Boelts
- *Tight Times* by Barbara Shook Hazen
- *Uncle Willie and the Soup Kitchen* by DyAnne DiSalvo-Ryan

Each year Jennie hosts a wedding between the letters *Q* and *U* (a common event in some K–1 classrooms to help children understand the use of these letters that "stand together" in words). She decided to extend the study of family identity to include an exploration of weddings as one way to form a family. Traditionally, a male and female student perform the role-play of the wedding between *Q* and *U*. By sharing stories and creating a context in which any student can participate, regardless of his or her gender, we send the message to students that anyone can get married and can love each other, thus leading to greater acceptance of various family structures.

Jennie read aloud *Lilly's Big Day*, which led to a conversation about all the jobs that have to be done when two people get married. The next day her read-aloud, *The Flower Girl Wore Celery*, opened up the discussion to marriage equality. When Jennie and her students reflected on the two stories, they noted that weddings are celebrations of the love between two people and these can be a man and a woman, a woman and a woman, or a man and a man, because, as one student put it, "love is love."

Other books focused on the theme of inclusivity and love of everyone include *Donovan's Big Day* by Lesléa Newman and *Worm Loves Worm* by J. J. Austrian.

To culminate this portion of the exploration of family identity, Jennie invited a few families of students in the class to share stories of their weddings. Following the readings and conversations, the students created "Love Is Love" signs, as seen in Figure 1–2.

Following the wedding of *Q* and *U*, Jennie and her students had a conversation about ways other than a wedding to make a family.

Jennie then read *Black Is Brown Is Tan* and extended the conversation about what makes a family. The students noted that the outside identity of this family shows one mom and one dad and their kids. They noticed that the parents have different skin tones, and a few children commented that this reflects their own families.

To explore family identity a bit further, Jennie read *Visiting Day*, which led to an interesting conversation about prison and how families sometimes don't live in the same house. This

A LOOK INTO THE CLASSROOM

Administrative support is essential to successful school initiatives. Join a conversation with Lester, Katie, Buffy Fowler, and Elana Froehlich about the importance of this work. Buffy offers great suggestions for enlisting the support of parents.

FIGURE 1–2 "Love Is Love" Sign

is an important mirror for children who have separated parents, a parent deployed in the military, or an incarcerated parent—and perhaps a more important window for children living in a more "traditional" family structure. As a result of reading this collection of books, Jennie's students concluded that a family is not necessarily the people who live in your house; a family is the people who live in your heart.

ALTERNATE GRADE EXAMPLE
First Grade

First-grade teacher Britney Ross read *Thunder Boy Jr.* by Sherman Alexie to explore the pros and cons of being named after a parent and having a nickname that you may not like. The book speaks to the power of a name and personal identity. She then read *My Name Is Sangoel* by Karen Lynn Williams and Khadra Mohammed to get readers to think about the power of a name and how a name is an important aspect of identity. Bringing the study to a close, she selected *My Name Is Bilal* by Asma Mobin-Uddin to open the conversation about acceptance and fitting in. This title lets us explore the impact of societal norms and expectations as they relate to personal feelings about one's name, culture, and religion as aspects of identity.

Students made the connection that in each of the first two stories the main character's name was very important. Thunder Boy felt his name limited him in becoming his truest self. Sangoel, on the other hand, was proud of his name because it was all he had. His name was his connection to the home he had to leave. He wanted to make sure everyone knew how to say it correctly, so he made a shirt to help the kids at his new school pronounce it.

As conversations about identity and the importance of a name continued, Britney brought in the third book, *My Name Is Bilal*. She asked students to think about the main character, Bilal, and how he was his truest self.

STUDENT: He was standing up for the person who was bullied.

BRITNEY: He did stand up for his sister. Remember, the book says, "Bilal took a deep breath. 'My name is not Bill. It's Bilal. My sister and I are Muslims,' he said stepping between Scott and Ayesha. 'And America *is* our country. We were born here'" [Mobin-Uddin 2005]. So how was he his truest self?

STUDENT: He felt proud of his name because he learned it was important.

STUDENT: He was proud of who he was and proud of his sister. He is American, but he knows his name is important.

STUDENT: And he is proud he is a Muslim, so he wants to use his Muslim name and not make up an American name.

Britney's students recognized that unlike Thunder Boy or Sangoel, Bilal was worried about what other people might say or how they might treat him because of his name. And like both other boys, Bilal realized his name was part of his identity. When a teacher helped him discover power and purpose in knowing the importance of his name, Bilal stepped into his truest self.

CONSIDERATIONS FOR THE **3–6 Classroom**

Here are some additional books that explore characters that experience tensions or struggles with their names when moving to a new country:

The House on Mango Street by Sandra Cisneros
My Name Is Yoon by Helen Recorvits
My Name Is Maria Isabel by Alma Flor Ada
The Name Jar by Yangsook Choi
Sumi's First Day of School Ever by Soyung Pak

These books offer cultural perspectives that could be discussed as a way to celebrate cultural differences. In addition, they can launch conversations to begin peeling back layers to address cultural bias. Ask students to consider these questions:

- Do you think people are treated in a particular way because of their name?
- Have you been treated differently because of your name?

If you, as a teacher, are interested in the opportunity to explore your own bias, you may want to check out a helpful resource from Teaching Tolerance at www.tolerance. org/professional-development/test-yourself-for-hidden-bias.

FOR YOUR CLASSROOM
The Stories Behind Our Names

Write about your own name. As you prepare to write, you may want to consider these questions to guide your thinking:

- Who selected your name?
- How was the decision made to name you this?
- Are you named for someone? Some place? Something?
- Does your name have a significant meaning that was part of the decision?
- How do you feel about your name?
- Have you ever considered changing your name? Why or why not?
- What other names were considered for you?
- What would your name have been if you had been born the opposite gender?

Consider sharing your own name story with your students as a way to share your identity and create community while also providing a model as a mentor text. You may also want to consider ways to extend this activity to facilitate oral and written language development through family connections. In what ways can students interview their parents and guardians to learn more about the history of their names? Consider the use of digital platforms such as Flipgrid, VoiceThread, or Book Creator to create an online space where students and families can share stories about their names using multimodalities. You could also host a family event at the school or a local community center where the children and their families share about their names, their heritage, and their cultures.

To learn more about ways to learn about each other's stories, visit My Name, My Identity at www.mynamemyidentity.org/ and take a pledge to pronounce students' names correctly.

Suggested Resources

PICTURE BOOKS
Ada Twist, Scientist by Andrea Beaty
Amazing Grace by Mary Hoffman
The Big Red Lollipop by Rukhsana Khan
Black Is Brown Is Tan by Arnold Adoff

The Blacker the Berry by Joyce Carol Thomas

The Boy Who Grew Flowers by Jen Wojtowicz

Chocolate Me! by Taye Diggs

The Colors of Us by Karen Katz

Dancing Home by Alma Flor Ada

Donovan's Big Day by Lesléa Newman

Drum Dream Girl by Margarita Engle

The Flower Girl Wore Celery by Meryl G. Gordon

Golden Domes and Silver Lanterns by Hena Khan

Grace for President by Kelly DiPucchio

The Highest Number in the World by Roy MacGregor

I Am Jazz by Jessica Herthel and Jazz Jennings

I Am Me by Karla Kuskin

I Love My Hair! by Natasha Anastasia Tarpley

I Love Saturdays y domingos by Alma Flor Ada

I, Too, Am America by Langston Hughes

Introducing Teddy by Jessica Walton

Isabella: Girl in Charge by Jennifer Fosberry

Jacob's New Dress by Sarah Hoffman and Ian Hoffman

Jalapeño Bagels by Natasha Wing

Jin Woo by Eve Bunting

Juana and Lucas by Juana Medina

King and King by Linda de Haan and Stern Nijland

King and King and Family by Linda de Haan and Stern Nijland

Let's Talk About Race by Julius Lester

Lilly's Big Day by Kevin Henkes

Looking Like Me by Walter Dean Myers

Mango, Abuela, and Me by Meg Medina

Marisol McDonald Doesn't Match / Marisol McDonald no combina by Monica
   Brown

Mixed Me! by Taye Diggs

Mommy, Mama, and Me by Lesléa Newman

Morris Micklewhite and the Tangerine Dress by Christine Baldacchino

My Brother Charlie by Holly Robinson Peete and Ryan Elizabeth Peete

My Name Is Aviva by Lesléa Newman

My Name Is Bilal by Asma Mobin-Uddin

My Name Is María Isabel by Alma Flor Ada

My Name Is Sangoel by Karen Lynn Williams and Khadra Mohammed

My Name Is Yoon by Helen Recorvits

My People by Langston Hughes

My Princess Boy by Cheryl Kilodavis

The Name Jar by Yangsook Choi

The Paper Bag Princess by Robert Munsch

Poems in the Attic by Nikki Grimes

Red: A Crayon's Story by Michael Hall

The Red Blanket by Eliza Thomas

René tiene dos apellidos / Rene Has Two Last Names by René Colato Laínez

Rosie Revere, Engineer by Andrea Beaty

Shades of People by Shelley Rotner and Sheila M. Kelly

Skin Again by bell hooks

Sleeping Bobby by Will Osborne and Mary Pope Osborne

Spaghetti in a Hot Dog Bun by Maria Dismondy

Sparkle Boy by Lesléa Newman

Spoon by Amy Krouse Rosenthal

The Story of Ferdinand by Munro Leaf

This Is the Rope by Jacqueline Woodson

Three Hens and a Peacock by Lester Laminack

Three Names of Me by Mary Cummings

Thunder Boy Jr. by Sherman Alexie

Two Mrs. Gibsons by Toyomi Igus

Visiting Day by Jacqueline Woodson

When Jo Louis Won the Title by Belinda Rochelle

William's Doll by Charlotte Zolotow

Worm Loves Worm by J. J. Austrian

Yo Soy Muslim by Mark Gonzalez

Zero by Kathryn Otoshi

CHAPTER BOOKS

Absolutely Almost by Lisa Graff

Brown Girl Dreaming by Jacqueline Woodson

Counting by 7s by Holly Goldberg Sloan

El Deafo by Cece Bell

George by Alex Gino

The House on Mango Street by Sandra Cisneros

One Crazy Summer by Rita Williams-Garcia

P.S. Be Eleven by Rita Williams-Garcia

Wonder by R. J. Palacio

ONLINE TEACHER RESOURCES

Perspectives Texts, searchable library of short texts from Teaching Tolerance, www.tolerance.org/classroom-resources/texts

CHAPTER 2

Making Unlikely Friends

I've learned that people will forget what you said,
people will forget what you did,
but people will never forget how you made them feel.

—Carl W. Buehner

To have a friend and be a friend is what makes a life worthwhile.

—Unknown

Who would expect a spider and a pig to become the best of friends? It is not a likely match, yet there is no greater friendship than the bond between Charlotte and Wilbur in E. B. White's classic children's book *Charlotte's Web*. We never know who may become a friend during our lives. The formation of a friendship is both mysterious and fascinating. There are the likely candidates, those who share our interests and those who are like us in many ways. Some of our earliest friendships are often orchestrated by parents and caregivers. Our first friendships may well be formed based on convenience. For example, a toddler's first friend may well be the child of a parent's friend. Friendships begin with interaction and are more likely to develop when we share space and ideas and stories. Our shared stories open a pathway to finding our overlapping interests and our intriguing differences. Our shared stories make us known and vulnerable, and this requires a level of trust and respect not often afforded to a general acquaintance. When trust, respect, and vulnerability are returned, we are even more likely to develop the connections that lead toward a lasting friendship.

In Mem Fox's beloved picture book *Wilfrid Gordon McDonald Partridge*, the friendship between young Wilfrid and elderly Miss Nancy, who lives next door in the old people's home, may well be considered unlikely. However, Wilfrid treasures her above all the other residents because she has four names just as he does. He visits her often and comes to know her well. When his parents comment that she is a "poor old thing" because she has lost her memories, Wilfrid translates his empathy into action.

This unlikely friendship becomes a model for readers of any age, demonstrating what unconditional love is.

The focus for this chapter is forming those unlikely friendships. The teachers and students featured here are reading and exploring the unlikely friendships revealed in selected texts. Our hope is that we lead students toward the understanding that friendships formed beyond the typical expectations are rewarding and often lasting.

Voices from the Classroom

This is both a new year and a new position for Kim Anderson, a third-grade teacher at Sterling Elementary in the Nicholtown community of Greenville, South Carolina. As a newcomer to the community, her only knowledge of Nicholtown came from news reports and hearsay. Knowing that, she sought to learn more about the community firsthand by making home visits to get to know her students and their families and by attending the Nicholtown community meetings to form relationships with members of the community. See Figure 2–1 for Kim's sample parent letter.

Home Visits—Fall Conferences

Hello Families,

I can't believe it is already time for conferences! I do conferences a little differently than many teachers because over the years I have found a very powerful way to connect families, students, and teachers. Most of you have heard me say that I believe in a team. Children need to know that *we are all in this together* and that *we* are *their* advocates and support system as they navigate their way through school. One way I show my students that I am on their team is by giving out my phone number. Many of you have it, but if you don't it is (XXX) XXX–XXXX. I tell students and families to stay in touch with me—not just this year, but in years to come. Let me know your successes in life and also how I can help. I spend an entire year with these sweet souls and love to hear how they are doing along the way!

Another way I show students that we are a family is through home visits. These are intended not to infringe upon your space but simply to connect school to home. Students LOVE when I come to their home. They are so proud of where they live and they are SO PROUD of YOU. I will only pop in for a few minutes and I will bring some goodies to help them reach their goals for the year. The last way that I show your children that we are in this together is by giving them ownership of their school experience through student-led conferences. When I come to your home, I will bring a sheet that your child has filled out, letting you know his or her glows (strengths) and grows (weaknesses). In third grade we are working toward independence, and accountability is so important.

Please sign up for a home visit below and return this form ASAP so we can work out any scheduling issues. I have really enjoyed these sweet kiddos so far and I look forward to seeing you soon!

Sincerely yours,

Kimberly Anderson

FIGURE 2–1 Kim's Parent Letter About Home Visits

Hear a community organizer in Nicholtown speak on the importance of partnerships between the community and the school.

She discovered that Nicholtown was Greenville's first black community. Its history dates to the mid-nineteenth century and it was once home to a diverse population of African Americans. Resident Sylvia Palmer noted, "This neighborhood, back in the forties, fifties, sixties, was a very good neighborhood, with a very diverse socio-economic level of African Americans. We had the poorest of the poor, the middle class, and common laborers. We had a lot of prominent schoolteachers, principals, preachers, and professional people as well. It was a very peaceful neighborhood. We all got along" (Davis 2016).

Over the years, this community has faced increased crime and infiltration of drugs, making some feel unsafe. In 2016, a shooting death of a Greenville police officer led to increased racial tensions. The people of Nicholtown remain at the heart of the community and actively seek to improve community relations and their reputation in the larger community. Upon learning more about the people who reside in Nicholtown and call it home, Kim set out to forge unlikely friendships within and across the community. Like Wilfred Gordon, the children in Kim's class made friends with local residents in an attempt to return to the peaceful community Nicholtown once was.

According to Delores Durham, president of the Nicholtown Neighborhood Association, "As a community, we strive for all of our children to work toward empowerment to uplift the community because any time a child has fallen short of that, we all lose" (Davis 2016).

Selection

Kim's goal was to empower students to build relationships within and beyond the classroom. She knew this would help create community and foster unlikely friendships. Each decision Kim makes, from setting up her classroom to include students' photos to the selection of a variety of texts, helps students explore themselves and the larger community. See Figure 2–2 to see how Kim displays student photos to create community.

The first read-aloud was *Momma, Where Are You From?* by Marie Bradby. After reading, Kim shared her own poem modeled after George Ella Lyon's poem titled "Where I'm From." See an excerpt of Kim's poem in Figure 2–3. Sharing her poem helped her students get to know her better and provided a mentor text for their own poetry. By example, Kim sets high expectations, demonstrates vulnerability, shares a range of emotions, and offers personal examples that allow children to ask questions or seek more information.

FIGURE 2–2 Student Photos Help Create a Sense of Community

I'm from long tables filled with boisterous personalities and vibrant laughter.

I'm from footie pajamas, warm snuggles, and making that one extra person fit perfectly on the couch.

I'm from hamburger steak, green beans, and mashed potatoes with au jus from S&S on Sundays after church.

I'm from Dillard's peaches cut up and served with milk for breakfast and hot Krispy Kreme doughnuts when the light comes on.

I'm from deep loss that has left holes in my heart and a pit in my stomach.

I'm from genuine love that comes from the Lord and also through the jovial, heart-felt daily interactions that fill my soul.

I'm from "Melody," "Recuerdos de la Alhambra," and "Una limosna por el amor de Dios" played by my favorite musician.

I'm from the Beatles, Simon & Garfunkel, Queen, and Michael Jackson, and *Hairspray* on long road trips.

I'm from "It Is Well with My Soul" even if it's not well with my mind.

I'm from molding my perspective through travel, deep relationships, and an open heart.

I'm from "no," "too little," "too much," and "not yet."

I'm from "I believe in you," "I'm proud of you," and "never give up."

I'm from "Will you marry me?" at my favorite place in the world.

I'm from becoming a mother in different hospitals, different states, and even through different bodies.

I'm from being the teacher and the learner all in the same day . . .

I'm from seeing the hurt, feeling the pain, and being the change one day, one experience, one relationship at a time.

That's Where I'm From.

FIGURE 2–3 Kim's "Where I'm From" Poem

Kim's students spent multiple days writing and creating multimodal poems to describe themselves and where they are from. Figure 2–4 shows one student engaged in the writing process and Figure 2–5 is an example of a student poem.

FIGURE 2–4 (below) Student
Preparing His "Where I'm From"
Poem for Publication

FIGURE 2–5 (right) Student Sample
of "Where I'm From" Poem

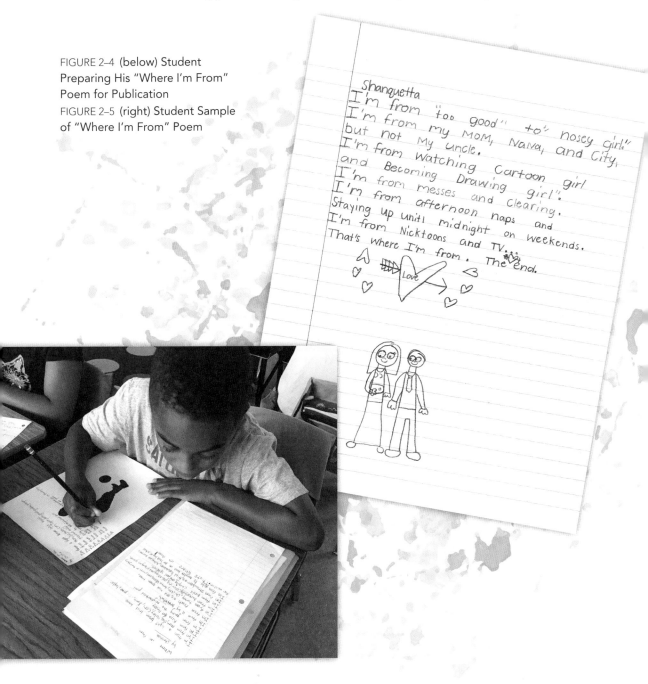

Shanquetta
I'm from "too good" to "nosey girl"
I'm from my mom, Nana, and city,
but not my uncle.
I'm from watching cartoon girl
and becoming Drawing girl".
I'm from messes and clearing.
I'm from afternoon naps and
Staying up unitl midnight on weekends.
I'm from Nicktoons and TV.
That's where I'm from. The end.
Love

FOR YOUR CLASSROOM
A Series of Writing Lessons

Notice how Kim provided mentor texts in the form of a picture book and a well-known poem as well as a poem she wrote. Throughout this process, Kim uses mentor texts to serve as a model for her own writing, she demonstrates writing in front of her students, and she writes in a way that allows her students to know her better. Think about applying some of Kim's strategies in your own writing lessons. You might

- show how a mentor text inspires your own writing
- demonstrate writing in front of your students to show that teachers are writers too
- share your thinking process as you draft before you ask students to write
- allow your writing to serve as a window for students to get to know you better.

Poetry often alludes to ideas through metaphors that require a reader to infer. It may leave the reader with questions that open communication. The contents of these poems allow us to get to know each other better and form friendships.

Kim extended the discussion to nudge students beyond the "Where I'm From" poems and to their role in the broader community. She selected the follow-up read-aloud, *Blue Sky White Stars* by Sarvinder Naberhaus, to help students consider how it may feel to be an immigrant coming to a new community. She selected a third book, *Music for Alice* by Allen Say, to help students empathize with a character who was not accepted into the community because she was Japanese American. Before reading this story aloud, Kim explained that during World War II there were Japanese American people who were U.S. citizens living in the United States. However, when the Japanese bombed Pearl Harbor, many people in the United States became scared and demanded that all Japanese American citizens be forced from their homes and placed in internment camps.

CONSIDERATIONS FOR THE **K–2 Classroom**

Although Kim teaches third grade, many of her read-aloud selections and writing lessons are appropriate for primary students, with some adjustments. In the younger grades you can stick to verbal responses to text. If you want students to respond in writing, demonstrate how writers sketch or draw their ideas.

Connection

As Kim read *Music for Alice* to her students, they made connections with the characters and empathized with the experiences of those characters.

> **KIM:** I want you to put yourself in the characters' shoes. Has there ever been a time in your life when you felt the way they did? Think about a time when somebody thought differently of you based on the way you looked–your clothes, your shoes, your hair, maybe your skin. Think about a time when you heard somebody say something negative or mean about your family.

> **STUDENT:** I was sad when I was playing outside. Somebody talked about my mom.

> **STUDENT:** Every time I go to my grandma's house, my sister talks about me.

> **STUDENT:** When I was in 4K at this school, Enzo was my best friend and he helped me by standing up to my bullies. I just wanted to be their friends, so I kept trying and then we were friends! It took me two years, but now I have so many friends!

After her students made personal connections, Kim asked them to think about how other people might feel.

> **KIM:** Consider how others would feel if we responded in similar ways. I'm never going to say mean things, because I know this would make me feel rotten if someone did it to me. It does not feel good when people say mean things, so I'm not going to say mean things about other people. We can use our words and tell them we don't like it when they say things like that to us.

> **STUDENT:** We can use our hearts and our words.

> **STUDENT:** We can create relationships with people.

Kim brought the conversation back to the book *Music for Alice* by summarizing the experiences Alice and her family faced as Japanese Americans. She pointed out, however, that once Alice's family was released from the internment camp, they had their own farm and treated the workers on their farm respectfully—"the way they would want to be treated" (Say 2004). She asked students to consider how the family's experiences at the beginning of the story influenced the way they then treated other people at the end of the story.

> STUDENT: They didn't want them to feel like them. They were putting themselves in their shoes.

> STUDENT: It's kind of like the book called *The Other Side*.

> STUDENT: It was like the neighbors were being mean to the black people but in *The Other Side*, the black girl–her friends were being mean to the white girl. The white girl asked if she could play with her, but the black girl's friends say no.

Kim had read *The Other Side* by Jacqueline Woodson prior to reading *Music for Alice*. *The Other Side* created a scaffold because students could more easily connect to the historical context of the plot.

As the conversation continued, the students made connections with many other books. For example, when reading *We're All Wonders* by R. J. Palacio, Kim invited the students to consider different scenarios.

> **KIM:** If you were walking down the street and you saw someone much older than you or someone whose skin was different, how would you respond?

> STUDENT: There's a guy on our street with a fake leg and people talk to him.

> STUDENT: I don't know if I'd talk to him. I might feel weird.

> STUDENT: I think we should say hi or how are you doing.

[Most of the kids agree.]

> **KIM:** Would you play with a person with an artificial limb?

> **STUDENT:** If you could have fun playing with someone else, you can have fun playing with him.

Kim's decision to read *We Are All Wonders* helped draw children's attention to our similarities rather than our differences.

FOR YOUR CLASSROOM
Character Anchor Chart

Depending on your students' experiences, review how the characters felt and what made them feel that way. Create a two-column anchor chart that lists character feelings on the left and the events that caused those feelings on the right. Follow up by asking students to consider a time when they experienced something similar. You might even add that to a third column.

Reflection

Kim revisited some of the texts she read aloud. She directed her students to think about the characters and how each of the characters reacted to the situations in the plot. Her goal was to help her students use the theme of making unlikely friends as a lens to make connections across the set of texts. She asked them to consider how each character felt and suggested they might try to write a "Where I'm From" poem from the perspective of one of the characters. See Figure 2–6 for a sample of a "Where I'm From" poem written from the perspective of the character from *Drum Dream Girl* by Margarita Engle.

The class discussed the importance of getting to know each other better by building relationships and extending that idea into the broader community. This is important within their own community of Nicholtown, as the area continues to experience poverty, crime, and ongoing racial tensions. With Kim's guidance, the children considered actions they could take in Nicholtown to make it a better place for all.

Kim referred to other books, including *Drum Dream Girl*, and explained that examples from books can inspire us to reflect on our talents and can be our tools to help us make a difference in the world.

A LOOK INTO
THE CLASSROOM

Lester and Katie have a conversation with Kim's third-grade students.

The students had a discussion about making the world a better place and charted their thoughts. You can see the chart in Figure 2–7. They came to the conclusion that changing the world was a big task for third graders. So they considered how they might make a difference in their own way. The conversations led to discoveries about each other from sharing their "Where I'm From" poems. Kim asked, "Could the people in Nicholtown get to know us better if we shared our poems with them?" This led to a plan.

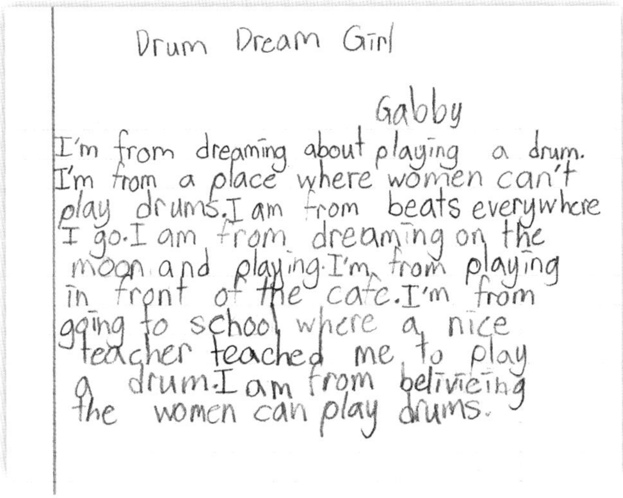

FIGURE 2–6 "Where I'm From" Poem Written from the Perspective of the Main Character from *Drum Dream Girl*

FIGURE 2–7 "Change the World" Anchor Chart

Action

Kim reached out to Delores Durham, the president of the Nicholtown Community Association, and secured a spot on the agenda of the upcoming community meeting. At the meeting Kim introduced the "Where I'm From" poetry project: "If you give kids their voice, if you let them talk, if you give them the tools they need, then they are able to share their stories. In the world, you don't have to watch the news to know there's so much violence and sadness going on. To be the change, we think it's important to have those real conversations with people and just really get to know people and invest in people." She explained that as a result of sharing their poems in class, students built relationships with their peers. They felt more comfortable and were able to have deeper conversations. They realized this was such a positive experience for them that they wanted to expand the project beyond their classroom and into the community.

Students shared their multimodal poems in the form of videos with voice-over, music, and images (you can see Jameeah's and Ty'Yez's videos at https://drive.google. com/open?id=1ZRCh-g3hLFXckHSf3cBmVDzY1RwQMNVs and https://drive. google.com/open?id=14ZS23_JhfE69VjzMtkX56kAvLDa1VTqC). The students then presented a brainstorming sheet and invited members of the community to write their own poems. See Figure 2–8 for the brainstorm sheet template.

Who are the people/pets who are important to you?	What does "home" look like? Do you live in a house, apartment, or somewhere else? Write down some details.
Are there certain foods that make you think of home?	Which activities make you think of home?
What do you hear at home or in your neighborhood?	Are there any smells that remind you of home?

FIGURE 2–8 "Where I'm From" Brainstorm Sheet

A follow-up meeting was scheduled so the community members could share their poems with the children. They hoped that sharing stories in the form of "Where I'm From" poems would help build relationships in the community. Figure 2–9 shows a photo of Kim with three of her students at the community meeting.

Kim selected texts as mirrors and windows for her students but was delighted to discover that the poems written by her students became windows into their lives. For example, when Montavious shared his poem, she gained deeper insights about him. Through his poem she learned that his dad had passed away last year. The last line of his poem read, "I'm from walking with my dad." Montavious decided this was one of the most important lines in his poem and chose to have the last image of his multimodal poem be one of him

FIGURE 2–9 **Kim talks with Tristian at the Community Meeting**

walking with a flyer commemorating his father's life (you can see Montavious' video at www.youtube.com/watch?v=I22bepIC4Ks &feature=youtu.be).

When he shared his poem at the community center meeting, Montavious proudly pointed to his shirt and proclaimed, "This shirt has got my dad on it." Figure 2–10 shows Montavious proudly wearing his shirt.

Notice how Kim continues to learn about her students through each phase of the process. Until the action phase, it was easy to assume that Montavious was referring to literally walking with his dad in his poem. Kim didn't know his father had passed away until she conferred with him about his poem.

After sharing at the community meeting, Montavious reflected on the experience: "It felt like I was opening up. It felt good to open up. I haven't opened up about it before, now that I think about it. I felt connected to my dad. An example is like

FIGURE 2–10 **Montavious at the Community Meeting Proudly Wearing a Shirt to Honor His Dad**

how I said we used to take walks. It felt very good. One thing about my dad is he loved music. I always used to listen to Michael Jackson. Me and my brother—one of my brothers on my dad's side—we'd always play the tape that my grandma had. We'd be dancing, and singing. [When I shared at the community center,] I saw some of my friends, [and the people from the church] were there. I liked it that my grandma came, and my little sister—well, one of my little sisters."

TAKE A MOMENT TO REFLECT

Pause and consider what you have learned about Montavious from reading his reflection. Now think about your students. What else can you do to make space for their voices in the classroom? Here are a few things you might consider:

> » Will your next read-aloud give students a deeper or different sense of friendship?
> » Do students have the opportunity to write and talk in a way that allows them to explore who they are and their role in the broader community?
> » Are there ways you and your students can be more connected to the community?

Jot down one thing you want to keep in mind as the school year progresses. ■

A police officer speaks about the importance of building relationships within the community.

According to Kim, "We feel if more people in the world would just start a conversation with somebody—if they would just have more conversations—then we would slowly get through some of these differences and just kind of unite together." Not only was this a powerful experience for the children who shared their poems, but it also helped them establish a connection with the community. Sharing our stories reveals our most basic human connections.

> *It is through shared story that we come to recognize where our lives overlap, where we stand apart from others, where we have some comfort to offer, where we can seek comfort. Story is a powerful force in humanity and children are wise enough to tap into it.*
>
> —Lester Laminack

Next Steps

A follow-up event was held at the school where students, their families, and community members came together to share a meal and present their "Where I'm From" poems. In Figure 2–11 Kim welcomes the families and explains the goals of the event. While sharing a meal, families read their poems with others at their table. After each poem was read, the poet highlighted a favorite line. These highlighted lines were woven into a collaborative group poem titled "Where We're From." In Figures 2–12a and 2–12b, students and their families work together to create their poems. Figure 2–13 shows a group taking its turn to read lines from its co-constructed poem for the larger group. You can read an example of a collaborative poem in Figure 2–14.

FIGURE 2–11 **Kim Welcomes the Community to the Event**

FIGURES 2–12a and 2–12b
Families Writing Poems

FIGURE 2–13 (above)
Families Sharing Poems

FIGURE 2–14 (right)
"Where We're From"
Community Poem

Where We Are From

We Are From Warm Big Blue-Berry Muffins. We are from big family with parents cousins, granparents and more. We are from EL-Amin, Crosby, Basketball, food, and a lot of laughter. We are from "Fly, Eagles, Fly."

I'm Katherine Thornton a Master hairstyles at Great Clips in Greenville SC.

I serve the commuinty by making sure that they hair look as best as it can.

We are from a warm house.

We are from the yellow house with brown shutters on Florida Ave.

We are from a loving family who blessings keep pouring in and we share with Love. Thank you God!

Inspired by Katherine Applegate's *Wishtree*, Kim and her class kept the momentum going and brought the new friends together once again to share their wishes for the future.

With the help of their teacher and their new friends in the community, these remarkable children used their words and actions to make their neighborhood a happier, more united place. As Kim reminds us, "You're never too young or old to make a difference in the world." You can see the video compilation of the "Where We're From" project at https://splice.gopro.com/v?id=VWXPMe.

ALTERNATE GRADE EXAMPLE
First Grade

Jessie Betten, first-grade teacher at Grove Elementary in Piedmont, South Carolina, read a collection of books focused on making friends. She began with Kevin Henkes' *Chrysanthemum*. After reading, she invited her students to consider which character reminded them of themselves and which character confused them. See the anchor chart in Figure 2–15.

One student stated that because her name is long just like Chrysanthemum's, she too was picked on in pre-K. Another said, "When I was in preschool I got picked on because I wore glasses. They'd say, 'Your glasses are so big, they look like heads.' They called me four-eyes. I closed my eyes and thought about dogs because they make me happy." This student later wrote about and illustrated this experience in the picture in Figure 2–16.

One student was perplexed that kids picked on Chrysanthemum just because she was named after a flower. The class discussed how kids shouldn't do that at school since school is like a family. A student commented, "And just like parents make us feel better when we are sad, we should make our friends feel better when they are sad." When asked who they would want to have a conversation with, students' responses included

o Which character would you like to know more about?
o Which character reminds you of yourself? Why?
o Which character do you admire?
o Which character puzzles you? Why?
o Which character would you want to have a conversation with? What would it be about?

FIGURE 2–15 **Character Anchor Chart**

FIGURE 2–16 Student-Written Reflection About Being Teased for Wearing Glasses

Chrysanthemum, her parents, the teacher, and the kids who were picking on her. One child said of those who were teasing, "I would have a conversation about being friends and would ask them to be my friend." Another said, "I would talk to the bullies. I would tell them she likes the name Chrysanthemum and not to pick on her."

After reading additional books, including *Stand Tall, Molly Lou Melon* by Patty Lovell and *The Recess Queen* by Alexis O'Neill, Jessie's students discussed ways to help people who are being bullied. They brainstormed how they could take action. Here are some of their ideas:

- We can write a note to tell them we are sorry you got picked on.
- We can write a book by stapling pages together to teach about how to help not get bullied.
- We can do an ad on TV that says help people stop getting picked on.
- We can make a commercial for the news at school.

Students collaboratively brainstormed, planned, drafted, practiced, recorded, and revised a PSA about bullying to share on the school news (you can see the video at https://drive.google.com/file/d/1G_P3G0RlVp53b8B-RQUxffsW3c3vfRUV /view?usp=sharing).

One student created an anti-bullying message using ChatterPix (you can see it at https://drive.google.com/file/d/1H-Lm7VTFJANuaH92uyoqB0loNpt5kxgc/view ?usp=sharing).

Suggested Resources

PICTURE BOOKS

The Adventures of Beekle: The Unimaginary Friend by Dan Santat

Amos and Boris by William Steig

An Angel for Solomon Singer by Cynthia Rylant

Bee-Wigged by Cece Bell

Big Al by Andrew Clements

Blue Sky White Stars by Sarvinder Naberhaus

Chrysanthemum by Kevin Henkes

Don't Be a Bully, Billy by Phil Roxbee Cox

Drum Dream Girl by Margarita Engle

Each Kindness by Jacqueline Woodson

Enemy Pie by Derek Munson

Finding Winnie: The True Story of the World's Most Famous Bear by Lindsay Mattick

Friends for Freedom: The True Story of Susan B. Anthony and Frederick Douglass by Suzanne Slade

Hello, My Name Is Ruby by Philip C. Stead

Hooway for Wodney Wat by Helen Lester

The Invisible Boy by Trudy Ludwig

Lailah's Lunchbox: A Ramadan Story by Reem Faruqi

The Lion and the Mouse by Jerry Pinkney

Listen to the Wind: The Story of Dr. Greg and Three Cups of Tea by Greg Mortenson

Llama Llama and the Bully Goat by Anna Dewdney

Momma, Where Are You From? by Marie Bradby

Music for Alice by Allen Say

The Orange Shoes by Trinka Hakes Noble

The Other Side by Jacqueline Woodson

The Recess Queen by Alexis O'Neill

The Sandwich Swap by Queen Rania Al Abdullah of Jordan and Kelly DiPucchio

A Sick Day for Amos McGee by Philip C. Stead

Smoky Night by Eve Bunting

Stand Tall, Molly Lou Melon by Patty Lovell

Those Shoes by Maribeth Boelts

We're All Wonders by R. J. Palacio

Who Was Martin Luther King, Jr.? by Bonnie Bader
Wilfred Gordon McDonald Partridge by Mem Fox

CHAPTER BOOKS
Because of Winn-Dixie by Kate DiCamillo
Charlotte's Web by E. B. White
Freak the Mighty by Rodman Philbrick
The Lions of Little Rock by Kristin Levine
Moo by Sharon Creech
The One and Only Ivan by Katherine Applegate
Raymie Nightingale by Kate DiCamillo
Wishtree by Katherine Applegate
Wonder by R. J. Palacio

CHAPTER 3

Coping with Loss

It has been a terrible, horrible, no good, very bad day.
My mom says some days are like that.

—Judith Viorst

Death leaves a heartache no one can heal,
love leaves a memory no one can steal.

—From an Irish headstone

There's no "should" or "should not"
when it comes to having feelings.
They're part of who we are
and their origins are beyond our control.
When we can believe that, we may find it easier
to make constructive choices about
what to do with those feelings.

—Fred Rogers

The words "coping with loss" likely evoke thoughts, images, or memories of the death of a loved one. However, the waves of emotions that follow a sense of loss are not limited to death, and adults are not the only ones who cope with those feelings. A child's first experiences with loss are more likely to be connected to a misplaced toy, a beloved stuff animal inadvertently left behind, a friend who moves away, or perhaps the death of a pet. Nonetheless, the emotions are there and the feelings are deep and unsettling. Of course, each of us knows students who have experienced terrible losses in their short time on this earth. It may be separation from a parent who is away in military service, a changed family structure due to a divorce, or a relocation that creates great distance from a beloved relative. The loss may be the death of a grandparent, parent, sibling, or classmate. Or it may have been the loss of a child's family home due to a disastrous event. Loss is never easy. Grief is painful and mysterious. Children most often lack the language and experience to express how they feel. They may be unable to articulate the tumultuous emotions they experience and the sense of dread and fear that arises out of nowhere.

Rather than avoid tough topics to protect our children from the hurt and heartache that come with the harsh realities of life, we should support them through these difficult experiences. We must help children cope with their raw emotions and help them understand that it is okay to show feelings and to lean on one another for support. In times when our country seems more divisive than ever, we must find ways to come together, to be connected, and to lift each other up. In an article titled "Why We Shouldn't Shield Children from Darkness" (2018), author Matt de la Peña tells the story of a young boy who moved the school auditorium to tears with his comment after de la Peña read his book *Last Stop on Market Street*. The boy said, "When you just read that to us I got this feeling. In my heart. And I thought of my ancestors. Mostly my grandma, though . . . because she always gave us so much love. And she's gone now" (de la Peña 2018). As he teared up, his friends leaned in and patted his back in support. This young man's unprompted response was brave and demonstrated his vulnerability. Yet not all children will feel comfortable to speak out and share their sadness, fears, and anxieties. And not all children will understand those emotions or have the words to express them. Therefore, we must create safe spaces for them to ponder, process, and feel supported.

In response to de la Peña's article, author Kate DiCamillo (2018) wrote about how her father's departure when she was a young child played a role in her decision to become a writer. DiCamillo recounts a particular school visit when one boy approached her at the conclusion of her presentation and confided that like her dad, his father also left. The boy said, "I thought I might not be okay. But you said today that you're okay. And so I think that I will be okay, too" (DiCamillo 2018). Kate's response: "You will be okay. You are okay. It's just like that other kid said: you're stronger than you know" (DiCamillo 2018).

This chapter delves into the human emotions of grief, sadness, and loss. Through a set of carefully selected texts shared by wise and empathetic teachers, children are able to explore the concept of loss. The read-aloud experiences paired with guided conversations give children the language to discuss their reactions, feelings, thoughts, and experiences in a safe and supportive setting. These texts may mirror the experiences of some children, providing them with both a sense of validation for how they feel and new ways to talk about them. For other students these texts are more likely to serve as windows that enable them to develop empathy with those who have experienced loss and cope with it daily.

Voices from the Classroom

In this chapter, we meet Andrea Phillips and her first-grade students at Wyandot Elementary in Dublin, Ohio, as they explore the topic of coping with loss. Andrea understands that children experience many changes in their young lives and are in transition between home and school and that this comes with letting go of security and consistent patterns. She understands that loss is defined in many ways, but she wants to give kids a chance to see that everyone has these feelings and situations in their lives.

They began with a read-aloud of *My Best Friend Moved Away* by Nancy Carlson and moved slowly through a collection of carefully selected texts. Join Andrea as she guides her students through conversations about coping with loss when a friend moves away and ultimately moves toward discussions about the experience of loss through the death of a loved one.

Selection

Andrea chose a set of books that would introduce her students to different types of loss. She wanted them to understand that humans react with a range of feelings when they experience any sort of loss, so some of the texts have a "happy ending" and some do not. Andrea made the texts available for independent reading and browsing. However, she chose to read aloud the following books to engage her first graders in whole-group discussions. Aware that she needed to move slowly into the topic of coping with loss, Andrea selected texts that were easy for her students to understand and relate to. She began with *My Best Friend Moved Away* and made careful decisions about what she would read next. Each subsequent title was selected based on what came up organically in the whole-class conversations. Other books included

- *Ida, Always* by Caron Levis
- *My Yellow Balloon* by Tiffany Papageorge
- *Nana Upstairs and Nana Downstairs* by Tomie dePaola
- *Rosie and Crayon* by Deborah Marcero

CONSIDERATIONS FOR THE **3–6 Classroom**

Just because your students are older doesn't mean they need more complicated texts. Sometimes when a topic is challenging, a simpler text feels easier to access and discuss. You may find these titles serve well as entry points into the discussion of coping with loss. If you wish to delve deeper into the topic, you may want to consider moving into one or more of these titles:

- *A Chair for My Mother* by Vera B. Williams
- *The Color of Home* by Mary Hoffman
- *Emmanuel's Dream: The True Story of Emmanuel Ofosu Yeboah* by Laurie Ann Thompson
- *14 Cows for America* by Carmen Agra Deedy
- *The Memory String* by Eve Bunting
- *A Shelter in Our Car* by Monica Gunning
- *A Storm Called Katrina* by Myron Uhlberg

CHAPTER BOOKS

- *Because of Winn-Dixie* by Kate DiCamillo
- *Charlotte's Web* by E. B. White
- *Esperanza Rising* by Pam Muñoz Ryan
- *Locomotion* by Jacqueline Woodson
- *The One and Only Ivan* by Katherine Applegate

Connection

During a whole-group discussion of *My Best Friend Moved Away*, a student commented that the girl "didn't get her friend back, but she got a new friend, even though they weren't the same, because nobody's the same." Spontaneously one student began singing the Girl Scouts' "Make New Friends" song and others quickly joined in. After the song concluded, one boy noted that the Cub Scout motto "Do Your Best" can also encourage you to make a new friend after one moves away.

Before reading *Rosie and Crayon* by Deborah Marcero, students used their knowledge of *My Best Friend Moved Away* and what they observed on the cover to make a prediction: "It might be like *My Best Friend Moved Away* because that girl loved her best friend and here, she's hugging her dog and maybe she'll lose him." After reading, students compared the two books and noticed "they both had something that went away that left them feeling sad, but they both made a friend at the end." Andrea guided her students to examine the role of the illustrations in *Rosie and Crayon* to help them notice how illustrations can be used to depict tone and mood. They noticed a change after Rosie's pup, Crayon, was gone: "Rosie is alone so the illustrator is making her world dark. She zipped her heart up so that no more love came out." Students observed how the illustrations became brighter as the story progressed, leaving the reader hopeful that Crayon might come back.

They discussed the role of the friendship in the other books and the importance of having people by your side when you need them. After reading, one student announced, "This is kind of like Rosie! Because they both had something that they liked, and then they all disappear."

FIGURE 3–1 **Sample of Student Writing About Loss**

Another responded, "It's like Martin Luther King because he died, and then his wife missed him." Students responded with their own feelings about missing someone or something through writing and drawing. See Figure 3–1 for a sample of student writing about loss.

Lesson on Responding to Text

Give students a chance to respond to text in some way. Andrea had already taught her first-grade students to respond through writing and drawing. You don't have to teach them a new way to respond. Apply what they already know. They might use any of these strategies:

- participate in a whole-group discussion
- talk to a partner
- record thinking on a sticky note
- write/draw in a notebook
- write/draw on a whiteboard
- write/draw on an iPad or other device
- record reactions on a video or audio app or website.

Andrea's students explored the varying emotions one has when coping with loss. When reading *Ida, Always* by Caron Levis, the students extended the feelings to include anger as a stage of grief. In the story, two polar bears named Gus and Ida are best friends. When Ida becomes deathly ill, they experience a range of emotions. Some days are growling days that involve anger. Other days are laughing days when they are happy doing things they love. Mixed-up days are days when "you can't tell which is which" (Levis 2016). Gus moves through a range of emotions as he mourns the loss of his friend Ida. One of Andrea's students captures the essence of the stages of Gus' grief: "Sometimes Ida's there and he's happy. Then when she died, he was mad. And now that Ida's gone, he's sad." Andrea's students explored the complexities and confusions associated with loss. One student commented, "Gus thinks he shouldn't smile or laugh because he's unhappy that his friend is dying." The students discussed the fact that Ida would always be in Gus' heart, that "she is in his love."

These conversations led Andrea to introduce another picture book. *Nana Upstairs and Nana Downstairs* by Tomie dePaola takes the concept of coping with loss a step further when the main character, four-year-old Tommy, struggles with the loss of his beloved great-grandmother (Nana Upstairs). Andrea read the book aloud to her students and asked them to pause a moment to think about the story. Then she asked the students to talk about what they noticed and what they wondered about.

> STUDENT: It reminded me of when my great-grandma died.

> STUDENT: My other grandmother's mom—she is my grandmother—when she was seventy-two she died because she had a heart attack.

> ANDREA: Raise your hand if this story made you think of someone you know and loved who died. Did you have any of the same feelings that Tommy did?

> STUDENT: I felt sad and a little angry because I only had one more grandmother left.

> STUDENT: Reminds me of when I was born, and a baby, my great-grandfather died.

Students not only shared stories of their loss but also shared how that loss made them feel.

Reflection

After initial reads of the texts, Andrea encouraged students to revisit them with greater introspection over the course of several days. After reading each book, Andrea asked students to help her summarize the story. They then moved into discussions as they related the book to other texts, events that had occurred at school, and students' connections and insights from beyond the classroom. Next, they examined the overarching message of the book and noted it on an anchor chart. With each additional book, Andrea helped her students notice commonalities across the texts. See Figure 3–2 for the book set comparison anchor chart. They summarized each book, noticed commonalities, and determined the broader theme across texts.

Next, Andrea asked students, "If you had a friend who was having all these different feelings because they were missing something, what would you tell them?"

Book	What was lost?	Feelings	Themes
My Best Friend Moved Away	her best friend moved away ◠	Sad bored angry dramatic / things got better!	made a new friend
Rosie and crayon	Rosie's dog got lost or died ◠	sad her world was colorless/dark / things got better!	Rosie made a new friend, found the cat
Ida, Always	Gus lost Ida, she died from sickness ◠	sad, mad, mixed up, growled, laughed / things got better!	he didn't have to see Ida to feel her
Nana Upstairs and Nana Downstairs	Tomie's 2 Nanas died ◠	sad, angry, Frustrated, curious / things got better!	he saw the shooting stars and felt nana in his ♡
My Yellow Balloon	He lost his balloon, it floated to the sky ◠	sad, crying, no color / things got better!	time made it better, the sun reminded him of his yellow balloon

FIGURE 3–2 Book Set Comparison Anchor Chart

The students recorded their thinking on sticky notes. See Figure 3–3 for a few examples of their notes.

While reading *Nana Upstairs and Nana Downstairs*, the students identified the tragic sense of loss Tommy experienced. They connected Tommy's feelings to their own struggles to make sense of the death of a loved one. Andrea picked up that thread and wove it into the broader fabric of the theme. She pointed out that losing a loved one—whether a pet, a family member, or a friend—leaves you with a sense of loss and sadness. She referred back to the way Tommy felt and reminded her students that reading a book like this helps us realize that we aren't the only ones who experience those feelings.

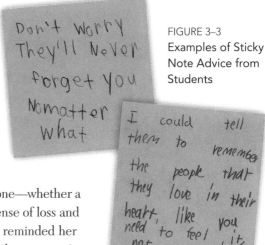

FIGURE 3–3 Examples of Sticky Note Advice from Students

Don't worry They'll Never forget you Nomatter what

I could tell them to remember the people that they love in their heart, like you need to feel it, not see it.

ANDREA: Do you see any connections between Tommy and any of our characters?

STUDENT: *Ida, Always*. The other bear was sad when Ida died.

STUDENT: All three of them. For Ida, Gus was sad. In *My Best Friend Moved Away*, she didn't die. She was confused. Their friends are gone.

STUDENT: They are all missing something.

ANDREA: When you are missing something or you've lost something, what do you do? How do you react?

STUDENT: Cry.

STUDENT: My cousin's brother moved away to college and he might never come back.

STUDENT: Sometimes I get angry and just want to stay in my bed.

STUDENT: When Tommy was sad, Gus was sad, and the girl was sad when her friend moved away, and Rosie was sad about her dog.

ANDREA: So you can have more than one feeling?

STUDENT: Yes. You can get nervous when you think about them. In your imagination you look at them in your window.

STUDENT: Angry and crazy like you just get angry so much that someone went away and you just throw everything down. The second thing, I can't remember the word, but like "overaction," like dramatic.

Notice how Andrea listens and scaffolds the connections and feelings, thereby making space for students' voices and ideas. She gently nudges the students toward taking responsibility and action.

ANDREA: Yes, sometimes we have strong feelings. When you are missing something and have these feelings, what can make you feel better?

STUDENT: Sometimes we can just talk to our family and friends when we are sad.

ANDREA: Yes, and we can talk to our school counselor. We can talk to our principal.

STUDENT: You can just let them cry for a little bit.

STUDENT: Just leave them alone.

ANDREA: Yes, sometimes people just need some space.

STUDENT: Play with them to help them get their mind off of it.

ANDREA: We are really good at this. If I was really sad about something, you are just the type of kids I'd want to be around, because look at all the ideas you have to help.

Andrea lists all the students' ideas on an anchor chart.

STUDENT: Sometimes you want to punch something, but you could get in trouble, especially if it's a person.

ANDREA: If you ever feel that way, let us know. Mr. Sprouse, the guidance counselor, has things in his office you can hit that won't hurt you or other people. He has things that will help you feel better when you are really angry and need to get your feelings out but don't know what else to do. We are realizing how important Mr. Sprouse is. He helps us express our feelings.

STUDENT: Mr. Sprouse has things we can squeeze.

STUDENT: He teaches us about feelings.

ANDREA: He wants us to understand that we will have lots of feelings in our lives and we need to find ways to handle our emotions. I wonder if there are things we can do to help people around school when they are missing something and have these feelings. Just like Mr. Sprouse, we would be good at it too. My brain is already filling with ideas.

In the course of the conversation, Andrea intentionally shifted the students' attention to Mr. Sprouse, whose job it is to help students make sense of and express their feelings. Andrea arranged for the class to visit his office, interview him, and get a tour. They learned about his job as a guidance counselor and his role in the school.

TAKE A MOMENT TO REFLECT

Andrea elicited the help of Mr. Sprouse. Think about the support staff at your school. Whom do you feel comfortable reaching out to? Make a list. You might also consider reaching out to community organizations for help or guidance. Be open to the ideas that come directly from your students. ■

Action

Just like Mr. Sprouse, Andrea's students were inspired to take action to help others who were coping with loss. Andrea asked her students to consider what they could do to help kids at their school who might be feeling sad or experiencing losses similar to those of the characters in the books they had been reading. Figure 3–4 shows a list of ideas the class brainstormed to help their friends feel better. The students decided to make a box with different items that Mr. Sprouse could use when students feel sad and come to see him.

> STUDENT: We could make games for his office. Make a box with different things like posters, jokes, cards, letters.

> STUDENT: We can write "From Team 118" on the front!

> STUDENT: So they know who cares about them.

> STUDENT: We have a ton of boxes already—we can make a walkie-talkie to connect whoever is sad with Mr. Sprouse so they can call him to come in.

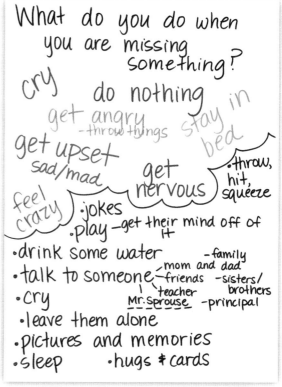

FIGURE 3–4 Student-Generated Ideas for How to Help Others Feel Better When They Experience Loss

It is important to point out that Andrea fully embraced this moment with her students. She allowed her students to be creative and be present in the moment, permitting them to delve into the action by just getting started right then and there. Andrea helped students get organized by having them make a plan and a list of materials they needed.

You can see students in the process of creating joke books, making stickers, and decorating a Feel Better Box in Figures 3–5 and 3–6.

The students proudly paraded to the counselor's office with the Feel Better Box in hand. They explained that the purpose of the Feel Better Box was to cheer kids up if they are sad. They showed Mr. Sprouse the things inside the box, including posters, jokes, stickers, and cheerful messages. They asked him to keep the box in his office since that is where kids go when they are sad and need someone to talk to.

FIGURE 3–5 **Student Creating a Joke Book Using a Mentor Text**

FIGURE 3–6 **Students Decorating a Feel Better Box**

Mr. Sprouse said that he had never had a class make a toolbox for him to use to help others. That really made the students excited. One student shouted, "We are changing the world!" And another replied, "Again!"

He asked if other kids could add to the Feel Better Box; they loved that idea. They especially liked to think that someone would use the box to feel better and then add to it something that had helped them or made them smile. Figure 3–7 shows the class presenting the Feel Better Box to Mr. Sprouse.

FIGURE 3–7 Giving the Feel Better Box to Mr. Sprouse

Next Steps

Andrea's students were so interested in the topic of coping with loss that they began to consider how additional texts fit within this theme.

> STUDENT: It's not a book we read yet, but I think we should read *Knuffle Bunny*.

> STUDENT: It's about this girl who loses a bunny in a hamper and she forgets that she put it there. Actually, everything but the people look like real-life things.

> **ANDREA:** Does that fit with the other books we've read?

> STUDENT: Yes, because she loses something. A bunny.

> STUDENT: **She gets it back, so it might be different.**

> STUDENT: **She gets sad and cries so loud.**

It is important to note that there are no one-size-fits-all books, book collections, lessons, or series of questions to guide these discussions. Rather, we want to consider our students as guides to the curriculum and use their input and curiosities as springboards for next steps in our teaching and learning, just as Andrea does in her first-grade classroom.

> *Grief is like the ocean; it comes on waves ebbing and flowing. Sometimes the water is calm, and sometimes it is overwhelming. All we can do is learn to swim.*
>
> —Vicki Harrison

ALTERNATE GRADE EXAMPLE
Third Grade

After Hurricane Harvey destroyed much of the Houston area in 2017, third graders in Kelley Layel's classroom at Wyandot Elementary in Dublin, Ohio, were filled with questions and concern for those affected. As a result, Kelley selected several texts, including *A Storm Called Katrina* by Myron Uhlberg and *Fly Away Home* by Eve Bunting, to explore what it feels like to lose something like your home. Next, they read articles like *Scholastic*'s "After the Storms," an interview about eight-year-old Lily Faith Johnston, who had to evacuate her home in Texas. The article also showed aerial photographs of the flooding in the Houston area. Kelley's students were inspired and brainstormed ways to help children in Texas cope with the loss of their possessions. Through social media, they connected with another third-grade class in the Fort Bend School District in Sugar Land, Texas. They collected money, school supplies, and gently used books and included letters to the students to explain how they wanted to help them recover from some of their losses. See Figure 3–8 for a photo of a sample student letter written in the child's native language of Japanese and translated into English.

This experience was empowering for these young children. They were particularly excited and over-whelmed when they received letters in return from the class in Texas. These third graders learned how small acts of kindness can help people cope with loss and make a difference in other people's lives.

FIGURE 3–8 **Student Letter**

Suggested Resources

PICTURE BOOKS

Bug in a Vacuum by Mélanie Watt

A Chair for My Mother by Vera B. Williams

The Color of Home by Mary Hoffman

Dog Heaven by Cynthia Rylant

Emmanuel's Dream: The True Story of Emmanuel Ofosu Yeboah by Laurie Ann Thompson

The Fall of Freddie the Leaf by Leo Buscaglia

Fly Away Home by Eve Bunting

14 Cows for America by Carmen Agra Deedy

Gentle Willow by Joyce C. Mills

Gifts from the Enemy by Trudy Ludwig

Ida, Always by Caron Levis

I'll Always Love You by Hans Wilhelm

The Invisible String by Patrice Karst

Knock Knock: My Dad's Dream for Me by Daniel Beaty

Knuffle Bunny by Mo Willems

Love by Matt de la Peña

The Memory String by Eve Bunting

Monday, Wednesday, and Every Other Weekend by Karen Stanton

My Best Friend Moved Away by Nancy Carlson

My Yellow Balloon by Tiffany Papageorge

Nana Upstairs and Nana Downstairs by Tomie dePaola

Nasreen's Secret School: A True Story from Afghanistan by Jeanette Winter

Papa's Backpack by James Christopher Carroll

Rosie and Crayon by Deborah Marcero

A Shelter in Our Car by Monica Gunning

Sophie's Squash by Pat Zietlow Miller

A Storm Called Katrina by Myron Uhlberg

The Tenth Good Thing About Barney by Judith Viorst

Thank You, Grandpa by Lynn Plourde

Visiting Day by Jacqueline Woodson

Wilfrid Gordon McDonald Partridge by Mem Fox

CHAPTER BOOKS

Because of Winn-Dixie by Kate DiCamillo

The Breadwinner by Deborah Ellis

Bridge to Terabithia by Katherine Paterson

Charlotte's Web by E. B. White

Death by Toilet Paper by Donna Gephart

El Deafo by Cece Bell

Esperanza Rising by Pam Muñoz Ryan

Hatchet by Gary Paulsen

Inside Out and Back Again by Thanhha Lai

Kira-Kira by Cynthia Kadohata

Locomotion by Jacqueline Woodson

The One and Only Ivan by Katherine Applegate

Out of the Dust by Karen Hesse

Pax by Sara Pennypacker

Tuck Everlasting by Natalie Babbitt

CHAPTER 4

Crossing Borders

Remember, remember always, that all of us,
and you and I especially,
are descended from immigrants and revolutionists.

—Franklin D. Roosevelt

Recognize yourself in he and she
who are not like you and me.

—Carlos Fuentes

***READING TO MAKE A DIFFERENCE* ONLINE RESOURCES**
To access the online videos for *Reading to Make a Difference*, either scan this QR code or visit http://hein.pub/ReadingToMakeADifference-login. Enter your email address and password (or click "Create New Account" to set up an account). Once you have logged in, enter keycode SPEAKFREE and click "Register."

Immigration did not end in the early to mid-twentieth century at Ellis Island. In fact, every year thousands of people continue to immigrate to the United States for a number of reasons. Across the world, some individuals are forced to literally cross borders to escape war, persecution, and violence in search of a better life. Whether a Sudanese refugee fleeing war or a Syrian refugee seeking asylum, each experiences hardships such as loss, loneliness, and inevitable danger. According to the United Nations, over 65 million people have been forced from their homes due to conflict or persecution. Approximately half of the world's refugees are children. Many leave their homes for work in another country, as is the case with many migrant workers who cross the border from Mexico to the United States. Natural disasters also result in the displacement of families. People are forced to leave their homes after earthquakes, hurricanes, tsunamis, wildfires, and floods. Displacement leaves children living in limbo as they and their families seek alternative shelter for indeterminate periods of time. Whether children in our classrooms and their families found shelter in a refugee camp, moved in with family in another town, or relocated to a new country, we must recognize that many of them are experiencing complicated realities. It is perhaps more important than ever that we teach about their realities accurately and offer our best support to all students, but especially to our undocumented students and English language learners. It is important that we move beyond the white European immigration story to create space for all students to see themselves in the immigrant experience (Sharma and Christ 2017).

This chapter explores the theme of crossing borders. The teacher and students featured here demonstrate how reading, talking, researching, and writing deepened their understanding of the plight of refugees across borders of time and geography.

A LOOK INTO THE CLASSROOM

Katie interviews Johnna.

Voices from the Classroom

Johnna Malici is the principal and fifth-grade teacher at a private Islamic school in Greer, South Carolina, where the students and their families are Muslim. She says that she chose to explore the theme of "crossing borders" because it "is personal and would appeal to [her] students." It also allows for a seamless integration of literacy, social studies, and technology. In addition, many of the countries that refugees are fleeing from are predominantly Muslim. Johnna strongly believes it is important for her students to see themselves and others like them reflected in the books they read.

> *I'm definitely going to do this again. It's been personally fulfilling [for my students] to read something with a real purpose behind it.*

—Johnna Malici, principal and fifth-grade teacher

Selection

While participating in the Global Read Aloud (theglobalreadaloud.com), Johnna's class read *A Long Walk to Water*, a dual narrative by Linda Sue Park. In this poignant story Park presents the true story of Salva Dut, a Sudanese Lost Boy, paired with the fictional story of Nya, a young girl from a warring tribe. In her effort to provide a more robust experience, Johnna selected a variety of articles, picture books, and poetry focused on the theme of crossing borders. The collection of texts provided a breadth and depth that no single text could. Students made connections with characters and events in the narratives, which served as a window into the lives of refugees.

Johnna was initially unaware of the number of books featuring refugees. She selected *Stepping Stones: A Refugee Family's Journey* by Margriet Ruurs because it is written in both English and Arabic. Johnna read the book in English and the Arabic language teacher at the school read it in Arabic. Johnna also added the book *My Beautiful Birds* by Suzanne Del Rizzo to present refugees through a more hopeful narrative.

CONSIDERATIONS FOR THE **K–2 Classroom**

Both of the picture books Johnna read aloud would be appropriate for younger students as well. *Stepping Stones: A Refugee Family's Journey* explains the plight of refugees in a dual-language (English and Arabic) text illustrated with beautiful stone images. *My Beautiful Birds* is written from a child's perspective with a hopeful tone. Here are some other books that might help young readers develop their understanding about refugees:

- *The Color of Home* by Mary Hoffman
- *Four Feet, Two Sandals* by Karen Lynn Williams and Khadra Mohammed

- *Lost and Found Cat: The True Story of Kunkush's Incredible Journey* by Doug Kuntz and Amy Shrodes
- *My Two Blankets* by Irena Kobald

Although Johnna included the chapter book *Refugee* by Alan Gratz for her fifth-grade class, she decided not to use it in its entirety. She selected the story of Josef, a Jewish boy living in 1930s Nazi Germany, because she hoped her students would see connections across persecuted groups. To bring a sense of reality to the stories, Johnna invited a friend to share her story about the persecution of her family by the Nazis during World War II.

Connection

As Johnna read aloud the story of Josef (from *Refugee*), she asked her students to examine the contrasts between Josef's life in Nazi Germany and his ocean voyage on the *St. Louis*. They quickly noticed his mischievous behavior while on board the ship and talked about how, unlike in his life in Germany, he was able to be more like a normal kid. They also noted that while on the ship Josef and his sister watched a movie for the first time, as Jews were not allowed in theaters in Germany. The students instantly made the connection between the segregation of the Jews in Nazi Germany with the segregation of African Americans in the United States. One student commented that the Nazis in *Refugee* reminded him of the Ku Klux Klan and their treatment of African Americans in the United States. He noted, "They [the Ku Klux Klan] used to come in their houses and trash everything and then kill them." Another student compared Josef's family's decision to escape Nazi Germany with the dilemma of Salva (*A Long Walk to Water*), who had to flee his war-torn country of South Sudan. "If Salva doesn't leave," the student observed, "he's going to die. And if Josef doesn't leave in fourteen days, he's going to die." These connections empower students with knowledge of the dire circumstances faced by many in the world who are forced to flee their homeland and seek asylum in a new country.

Johnna's class extended their connections through research to create infographics on refugees from different countries. They used student-friendly websites and took notes to determine why refugees were fleeing. Figure 4–1 shows a group of students searching for statistics and maps. Johnna supported the students' infographic work by providing a criteria list in Figure 4–2.

Johnna explained the importance of citing credible sources. To learn the research process, students initially used websites Johnna suggested. They quickly moved beyond those controlled search engines to explore other sites that required them to evaluate the credibility of sources.

FIGURE 4–1 (left)
Students Search for
Statistics About Refugees
Online

FIGURE 4–2 (below)
Infographic Criteria List

INFOGRAPHIC REQUIREMENTS

CRITERIA	NOT YET	ALMOST	YES!
Description of the Problem Why are refugees fleeing this area?			
Size of the Problem Use numbers and/or statistics to show how many refugees there are. When did refugees begin fleeing? How long has the problem been going on?			
Location of the Problem Include a map to show the affected area. Where are the refugees going? Include visuals, such as statistics (graphs) and maps, to present this information.			
Important Quote Include at least one quote from an expert or affected person that sheds some light on this situation. Be sure to introduce the quote.			
Solution to the Problem What can people do to help? What can governments do to help?			
Visual Display Create a visually appealing display. Be sure words are spelled correctly and sentences are complete and clear.			
Sources Cite at least two credible sources for your information.			

She reminded them to add the names of organizations in the context of their writing to make it more credible, even if they were paraphrasing. She demonstrated how to use citations with a sentence stem as a scaffold:

According to _____ and _____, "insert quote."

Johnna explained that the reader will pay more attention if they cite credible sources. She pointed out, "The reader will know he can trust the writing if experts like the Head of the UN Refugee Agency is cited." She also recommended that students edit their work throughout the process and again at the end before publishing the infographic. "The reader will not trust our writing if there are run-ons and spelling errors," she warned.

Notice how the work Johnna does with her students gives them the opportunity to refine and apply a number of skills such as note taking, synthesizing multiple sources, verifying the credibility of sources, and citing references. Johnna also reminds students that their writing must still follow the writing process of brainstorming, drafting, revision, and editing.

At the end of one class period, Johnna gathered the students together and invited them to share what they were learning about refugees.

STUDENT: They just went into the villages suddenly. They didn't have any time, they didn't have any warning, they didn't say "Go"; they just started fighting in the village and they started burning it.

STUDENT: It's because they're Muslim–that might be one of the reasons. And they're Jewish, so maybe it's about their religion.

STUDENT: In Syria and the countries where refugees are coming from, they either leave or they're going to die–they're going to be killed.

STUDENT: They're fleeing, and the government is forcing them out. Where are they going to go? If no one helps them, it's like a trap. Either you die out there and you have this very small chance to get accepted somewhere, or you die out there because of starvation.

Students' comments focused on the common experiences of refugees, even though the research was focused on specific groups of refugees from different countries. The read-aloud experiences coupled with the research project helped students connect to the plight of refugees. They also gained a deeper understanding and broader perspective. Johnna challenged her students to reflect on how their new insights changed their thinking about refugees.

Reflection

The students agreed that the most difficult part of Salva's journey was losing his family and having to travel so far barefoot. One group shared that they were surprised how the narratives of Salva and Nya intertwined at the end when Salva returned to his village to build wells that would provide clean water for the people.

> STUDENT: Both [Nya and Salva] live in South Sudan and have no water.

> STUDENT: It keeps you in suspense. Nya's story adds to Salva's because they both experienced sickness of a loved one because of dirty water.

> STUDENT: Both of them want healthy water.

> STUDENT: I think it is more interesting to see both sides of one story. They are both enemies, but both have to deal with water and have to walk to get water.

Students examined the use of the dual narrative to tell this story. They talked about the similarities between the two characters, specifically noting the important connection to water. They found it most interesting that even though Salva and Nya were members of two conflicting tribes, they shared common essential human needs.

The insight and empathy emerging from this fifth-grade conversation was remarkable. They expressed deep concern for Nya when they considered what it was like to walk so many miles every day to get water for her family while sacrificing the opportunity for an education. As students contributed their reactions to the significance of the title, *A Long Walk to Water*, they examined how Nya's life would change as a result of access to clean water.

> STUDENT: She had to walk every single day.

> STUDENT: At the end, she would be able to go to school because she didn't have to walk to water two times a day.

STUDENT: Now there's a well, so she has more opportunities.

STUDENT: Her life will be easier. If she goes to school, she can do more with her future.

The conversations and research that followed the read-alouds revealed new and more robust understandings of the plight of people without easy access to clean water. Johnna's students came to the conclusion that digging wells for local communities required resources and equipment beyond the reach of most people in Sudan. They discussed the relationship between access to clean water and community health and noted how the lives of everyone in the community would change for the better. Many students focused on the fact that girls like Nya would now be able to go to school since they no longer had to spend their days walking for water.

Another group reflected on the author's craft and how the clear descriptions allowed them to envision being in Sudan. The context helped them empathize with the hardships that Nya and Salva faced. The students explored how the book served as a window into a different way of life and allowed them to reflect on their own privilege.

STUDENT: I felt the author did a good job in her writing. She helped me understand how people live and feel in Sudan without being there.

STUDENT: Imagine how hard it must've been for [Salva] to stay in refugee camps for years and years. It's very hard, but when he left he had hope of getting to America, but he also thought now I'll never get to see my family. There's no hope.

STUDENT: Nya doesn't want to walk all day to get water, but she does. She doesn't walk to get the water for herself—she gets it for her family. She works all day long just to get water for her family. It's dirty water. And then when she gets there, there is a long line of people who want to get water. And it's disgusting. And she walks all day to get it. Imagine she drinks some and when she walks back it's bumpy and some of the water spills. It's heavy. When she gets home she has to go back again. That was really bad for her. Imagine doing school all day long and being so tired, and then imagine you get home, do homework, eat, and go right back to school.

The students' comments make it clear that this text provides a window into life in South Sudan and the plight of those with limited access to water. Their comments also reveal a nascent understanding of how a text serves as a mirror. They are trying to imagine themselves in the character's place.

On another day, Johnna read her students a poem titled "Home" by Warsan Shire. Her students made connections to their readings and discussions related to refugees. After multiple readings of the poem, students reflected on the powerful use of language and craft to create emotion and a sense of urgency felt by refugees.

> STUDENT: In the beginning, [Salva] was at school, and then he ran away. This is like this kid is running away from home or something, but to Salva, it just happened suddenly–he's just in class and all of a sudden there's gunshots and everybody's running away. That kind of connects to this part right here.

> STUDENT: It says, "no one leaves home except if home is like a shark . . . because I know that anywhere is safer than here" [Shire, n.d.; inaccuracies in the quotation reflect the student's statement].

> STUDENT: You can't go see your mom? That's really important to me. For us, every day we go home and you can see your mom. For them, it's like you can't even go there even if you wanted to. And "home is the mouth of a shark" [Shire, n.d.] stuff is still going on there really bad. And it says, "when the kid was holding a gun bigger than him" [Shire, n.d.; inaccuracies in the quotation reflect the student's statement] and the soldiers took him because the other group didn't even want him, they left him. Remember that?

> STUDENT: Because it puts more life in the writing to say that home is dangerous–it's like the barrel of a gun.

> STUDENT: It has more meaning to say "home is the mouth of a shark" [Shire, n.d.] than to say "home is dangerous." So when you use a metaphor in your writing, it makes your writing have more meaning. Especially in poems, they use more metaphors because poems are about meaning and rhythm.

Notice how the conversation focused on craft. What you don't see in this conversation is the rich and robust writing workshop that regularly occurs in Johnna's classroom. If literature serves as a window, it will provide a view to experiences, concepts, and language beyond our own schema and background knowledge.

FOR YOUR CLASSROOM
Studying Author's Craft

One way to explore books as windows is to study the author's craft. There are many different approaches to studying author's craft, but one way is to examine how an author crafts writing to help the reader develop empathy. In the book *Brave Girl: Clara and the Shirtwaist Makers' Strike of 1909* by Michelle Markel, readers learn that although it is difficult for recent immigrants to find work, young girls are hired for meager wages to make women's clothing and many take the jobs to help pay for food and rent for their families. Using this book or another selected historical fiction text, explore how the author develops empathy by using comparisons and contrasts, facts, and setting details. Following the study of author's craft, we would encourage students to then try out a particular type of craft in their own writing. The sample anchor chart provides three examples of different author's craft techniques from *Brave Girl: Clara and the Shirtwaist Makers' Strike of 1909* along with a description of how it helps the reader to develop empathy.

AUTHOR'S CRAFT TECHNIQUE	WHAT WE LEARN FROM THE TEXT	HOW IT HELPS THE READER DEVELOP EMPATHY
Comparisons and Contrasts	Instead of carrying books to school, many girls carry sewing machines to work.	It compares carrying machines to work to carrying books to school, something that most kids can understand.
Facts	There are two filthy toilets, one sink, and three towels for three hundred girls.	The specific numbers attached to familiar objects (toilets, sinks, and towels) allow readers to imagine how difficult the conditions must have been.
Setting Details	The sunless room is stuffy from all the bodies crammed inside.	It allows readers to picture the darkness and feel the confining and crowded nature of the factory.

To convey their understanding of the plight of the refugees they had been reading about, Johnna's students created blackout poems. They selected the page they felt was most significant to the story and made a photocopy of that page. Next, they used a pencil to draw boxes around key words and phrases. With this meaningful text selected, students then used a black marker to shade out the remainder of the text, leaving a poignant and powerful poem. Figure 4–3 shows a student working on her blackout poem and Figure 4–4 shows an example of a completed poem. The poet, Habiba, wrote that she is "trying to show through this poem that Salva's uncle was literally the key to Salva's life and that when there's so much stuff happening, take everything one step at a time."

Listen to fifth graders in Johnna's classroom engage in small-group discussions on the questions that intrigue them most.

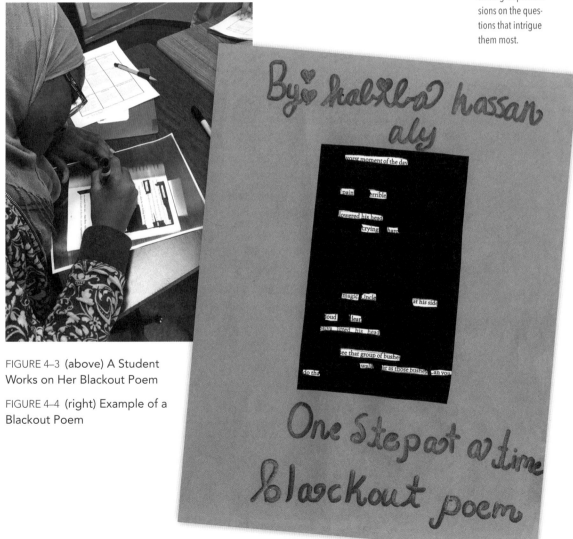

FIGURE 4–3 (above) A Student Works on Her Blackout Poem

FIGURE 4–4 (right) Example of a Blackout Poem

Action

Readers of A Long Walk to Water *see one person making a difference. And many of them have chosen to help. Students have donated over 2 million dollars—enough for more than 130 wells serving literally thousands of people.*

—Linda Sue Park, author of *A Long Walk to Water*

A LOOK INTO
THE CLASSROOM

Observe how Johnna and her students seamlessly weave their study of crossing borders into a new focus on developing unlikely friendships.

After several weeks of reading, discussing, and researching, Johnna asked her students to pause and reflect: "How are you different now that we have all these new insights and information? Does that new understanding nudge you to take some action, to do something that may help make the world a better place?" Together, the students brainstormed ideas for a refugee action plan along with the purpose for each idea (to educate, persuade, or act). Figure 4–5 shows the ideas they collected.

With an extensive list of ideas, Johnna's students narrowed the list to three action items. They considered the amount of time and effort needed to carry out the tasks and which tasks they believed would have the greatest impact. The students developed reasons and debated with their peers to ultimately make their decisions.

The students collectively decided to have a Refugee Week at school with a variety of activities culminating in a Walk for Refugees in the local community. Figure 4–6 shows the poster they created to advertise the walk. Johnna created a Facebook event to share with the wider community. Funds were donated to Islamic Relief USA's programs for refugees. They kicked off Refugee Week with a presentation for the school. Each student in the class participated by setting a scene to help the audience consider what it would be like to be a refugee, learn more about Salva's story from the book *A Long Walk to Water*, learn facts about refugees, and consider ways they could get involved through Refugee Awareness Week. A video of the presentation can be seen on the school's Facebook page (www.facebook.com/sabeel.academy/videos/1811869828825478/).

Refugee Action Plan

1. Presentation for the school using our skits, providing narrated stories and statistics from our infographic (Educate/Persuade)
2. Create a website (Educate/Persuade)
3. Have a Refugee Week at school
4. Write a letter to Brain Pop advocating for a video about refugees (Persuade/Educate)
5. Create a petition and collect signatures in favor of allowing more refugees in SC and send to SC legislators (Persuade)
6. Hold a water walk-a-thon. Get sponsors for each lap walked and donate the money collected to an organization that helps refugees (Act/Educate)
7. Donation boxes - ask the ISG Exec. committee if we can collect for refugees after Jumman Salah, have collection boxes in the school, etc. (Act)
8. Give 3 Campaign - encourage all students in the school to give $3 of their own money to help refugees (Act/Educate)
9. Car wash - work together to hold a car wash. All money collected would go to an organization that helps refugees (Act)

FIGURE 4–5 Refugee Action Plan Brainstorming List

WALK FOR REFUGEES!
There are over 65.3 million refugees.
They Need Us!

Get Sponsors. Walk. Help Refugees.
Register @ https://goo.gl/forms/
N9oKhf4jRHa1k6i23
Saturday, March 3rd
10:00 - 11:30
Cleveland Park Shelter 6
Next to Sand Volleball Court
**East Washington and Cleveland Park Drive
Greenville**
All funds will go to Islamic Relief programs for refugees.

FIGURE 4–6 Walk for Refugees Poster

Next Steps

On a beautiful spring Saturday morning in Cleveland Park near downtown Greenville, South Carolina, Johnna and her students welcomed the community to their Walk for Refugees. Doughnuts, cookies, water, and juice were generously donated by a local grocery store and a sub shop. The 1.5-mile walk was led by students, with student ambassadors located throughout the walk to point walkers in the right direction. Following the walk, participants returned to the park, where they had refreshments and listened to speakers. Three students recited the poem "Home" by Warsan Shire (you can see the video at https://drive.google.com/open?id=1GBT7t8RWseu7BXW u06mnkiDd1RJBwybP). Students raised $3,158.38, which was donated to Islamic Relief USA's programs for refugees. Figures 4–7 through 4–10 show moments from the walk.

AT LEFT:

FIGURE 4–7 (top) Johnna and Two Students Talk with the Local News About the Event

FIGURE 4–8 (bottom) Walk for Refugees

AT RIGHT:

FIGURE 4–9 (top) Students During the Walk

FIGURE 4–10 (bottom) Proceeds Were Donated to Islamic Relief USA

Banner reprinted with permission from Islamic Relief USA, www.irusa.org

TAKE A MOMENT TO REFLECT

As you move your students to take action, consider asking the following questions:

» How are we changed by what we have come to know?
» Does your new knowledge make you appreciate anything more?
» Are you more aware of any particular issue? How so?
» What can we do to help? ■

Technology enabled Johnna's students to gain access to information beyond the walls of their school. They used laptops to facilitate research, note taking, and the creation of infographics to teach others about the plight of refugees. Technology also allowed readers from around the world to connect digitally during the 2017 Global Read Aloud (GRA) to discuss *A Long Walk to Water*. Katie's undergraduate preservice teachers participated in the GRA and visited Johnna's class for real-time discussions. They also connected with a number of classes, including fifth graders in Lisa Stringfellow's class in Massachusetts and students in Angela Johnson's classes in Indiana. The blog post in Figure 4–11 demonstrates one student's understanding of refugees, her developing empathy, and her desire to take action as a result of reading *A Long Walk to Water* with readers from around the globe. Figure 4–12 shows another student's response.

FIGURE 4–11 (top) *A Long Walk to Water* Blog Post

FIGURE 4–12 (bottom) Peer Response to Blog Post

Blog post #5

By Leah on Nov 2

What new understandings do you have about the lives of refugees around the world?
What are some of the hardships Salva encountered on his journey to the refugee camps and while he stayed there? What are some ways Salva kept his hope strong while in the camps? How did he work to help others and improve himself?

These refugees do not get to pick what they go through, it's not a choice for them. They either die, or they have to keep on going by walking or living and keeping as safe as they can wherever they are. A new understanding I have about the lives of refugees around the world is that they can't controll what their going through. If it's a war, terrorist attack, hurricane, etc., they weren't the ones who had said yes to it, it just happened, they can't control it. Plus, it's really hard for them, "*I have been roaming around with my son for 60 days now,*" the women is the trailer of the movie, *The Human Flow* had said. They don' know where they are going to end up or live in the end. It's so sad to think that over 65 million people don't have anywhere to live, much food, or don't know where their family is. They could be alive, or dead. Some of the hardships Salva's encountered on his journey to the refugee camps and while he stayed there was that he had no family, he was a child with no family or friends, and was living in his own for over seven years. Some ways Salva's kept his hope strong while in the camps is just trying to get through each day. Like his uncle did when he hurt his toe, he's doing the same except saying that he just needs to get through that day, then the next, and so on. He worked to help others improve and himself was by being a very strong leader and always telling the younger ones what he always told himself. He helped others gat food and water and get to the refuges camp to get them safe. I feel very strongly and want to learn more about refugees and how to help them find homes, food, and water.

Abby

I loved this post! I agree with you that they either die or walk. I also feel strongly about helping anyone I can. How do you think you can help? I loved this and can't wait to read more!

Nov 9, 2:28pm

Angie Johnson posted to ▌**Mrs. Johnson's classes**
Teacher
Jan 3 · 11:13 AM

Ngun's response about a connection to Salva:

When I was in Burma there was a war like Salva, but us they burn our houses and village, and we had to run to the forrest and hide and we needed water and food but there were not that much water and food left but almost everyone survived and we had to stay in the cold for about 1-2 years, and while we were running, there were mostly kids my age like 2-3 years old and they had to give us Piggy back ride because we couldn't walk.

Unlike (1) · 1 Reply · Share · Follow

FIGURE 4–13 Ngun's Edmodo Response

Angie Johnson posted to ▌**Mrs. Johnson's classes**
Teacher
Jan 4 · 8:34 AM

Eden's response about a connection to Salva:

I want to write about how Salva has hope and I have a connection. My hope was to keep on trying until you accomplish what you want to accomplish. When I'm new to US, or when I came to US I don't understand what people were saying, and I don't know what to do at school, but I didn't give up. I kept on trying, by trying to talk to friends in English. And, I also kept trying hard by looking at dictionary. But one day I have to move away from my friends. (Best friend) I have to go to a new school, and I don't have anyone to talk to so, I just stay quiet until someone talk to me. I was brave enough to talk to her back. Now I accomplish my goal. I start talking even though I am not good. I over come my dream or goal by not losing hope.

Like · Reply · Share · Follow

FIGURE 4–14 Eden's Edmodo Response

Lisa's students used a variety of modalities to respond to the book. In a blog post, Karina presents a video to share her thoughts on the book, including the importance of water and how her empathy has led her to brainstorm ways to take action (you can see the video at https://kidblog.org/class/a-long-walk-to-water-global-read-aloud-2017/posts/6nw4zafqnbtvkak3h47gwjjpw).

Students in Angela's class considered how *A Long Walk to Water* served as a window and mirror for them through the written reflections they shared using the website Edmodo in Figures 4–13 and 4–14.

Participating in the Global Read Aloud showed readers that they are part of something bigger than themselves and that a book can connect us both near and far. To learn more about the Global Read Aloud visit www.theglobalreadaloud.com.

FOR YOUR CLASSROOM
Technology Can Enhance Learning

Technology can play an important role in helping students learn about other people's experiences. It can also give students a platform to share what they learn with a wider audience. However, it is essential that children learn to be critical consumers and producers of digital content. Just as we teach children to be good citizens in the classroom and in the community, we must also teach them to be digital citizens when in online spaces. Katie Stover (Kelly) and Lindsay Yearta (2017) suggest teaching minilessons to compare reliable and unreliable resources. They also recommend the 5 Ws for Web Evaluation:

- Who wrote the piece? What are the author's credentials?
- What is the purpose of this site? What information is included in this site?
- When was the site created? Last updated?
- Where is the information from?
- Why was this information written? Why is this page more useful than other websites? (Stover and Yearta 2017)

For more information, refer to the International Society for Technology in Education (ISTE) and state-level standards, as well as school or district guidelines for safe and responsible technology use.

ALTERNATE GRADE EXAMPLE
Fourth Grade

While Johnna's class and those reading *A Long Walk to Water* as part of the Global Read Aloud explored how crossing borders related to the forced displacement of refugees from their homes, Daniel Hoilett's fourth-grade class at Brushy Creek Elementary in Taylors, South Carolina, examined how Christopher Columbus crossed borders as he explored the new world. They moved beyond the traditional narrative of Columbus as a celebrated hero as they read Jane Yolen's *Encounter*. In this book, Yolen depicts the alternate narrative of Columbus' journey to the new world as told from the perspective of a young Taino boy. Daniel's students considered how Columbus used his power to enslave the Taino people and take their land. They discussed the importance of Yolen's version of the story as a counternarrative.

When asked whether they should celebrate Columbus Day, Daniel's students suggested alternatives like renaming it "So Much for Gold Day" because Columbus slaughtered the indigenous people for gold. Others simply stated that we should call it a "bad day" or "Monday" because "you don't want to celebrate someone who slaughtered people and killed off a tribe."

Daniel's students continued to learn about Columbus through song, video, and primary documents. They wrote about and debated the renaming of Columbus Day as Indigenous Peoples Day.

Conversations such as the ones in Daniel's classroom help students critically examine texts and the world. Through his intentional selection of text and facilitation of thoughtful discussion, Daniel's students connected to previous learning about explorers and extended their learning to question inequities and disrupt the commonplace.

Suggested Resources

PICTURE BOOKS

All the Way to America by Dan Yaccarino

Amelia's Road by Linda Jacobs Altman

Brave Girl: Clara and the Shirtwaist Makers' Strike of 1909 by Michelle Markel

Brothers in Hope: The Story of the Lost Boys of Sudan by Mary Williams

The Butterfly by Patricia Polacco

The Cat in Krasinski Square by Karen Hesse

The Color of Home by Mary Hoffman

A Day's Work by Eve Bunting

Dear Primo: A Letter to My Cousin by Duncan Tonatiuh

Encounter by Jane Yolen

Four Feet, Two Sandals by Karen Lynn Williams and Khadra Mohammed

Going Home by Eve Bunting

Grandfather's Journey by Allen Say

The Great Migration: Journey to the North by Eloise Greenfield

The Harmonica by Tony Johnston

Harvesting Hope: The Story of Cesar Chavez by Kathleen Krull

Henry's Freedom Box: A True Story from the Underground Railroad by Ellen
    Levine

How Many Days to America? A Thanksgiving Story by Eve Bunting

The Keeping Quilt by Patricia Polacco

The Little Refugee by Anh Do and Suzanne Do

Lost and Found Cat: The True Story of Kunkush's Incredible Journey by Doug
    Kuntz and Amy Shrodes

Mango, Abuela, and Me by Meg Medina

The Matchbox Diary by Paul Fleischman

The Memory Coat by Elvira Woodruff

Milly and the Macy's Parade by Shana Corey

Mirror by Jeannie Baker

My Beautiful Birds by Suzanne Del Rizzo

My Chinatown: One Year in Poems by Kam Mak

My Diary from Here to There / Mi diario de aquí hasta allá by Amada Irma Pérez

My Name Is Sangoel by Karen Williams and Khadra Mohammed

My Name Is Yoon by Helen Recorvits

My Two Blankets by Irena Kobald

The Name Jar by Yangsook Choi

One Green Apple by Eve Bunting

Pancho Rabbit and the Coyote: A Migrant's Tale by Duncan Tonatiuh

The Quiet Place by Sarah Stewart

So Far from the Sea by Eve Bunting

Star of Fear, Star of Hope by Jo Hoestlandt

Stepping Stones: A Refugee Family's Journey by Margriet Ruurs

A Storm Called Katrina by Myron Uhlberg

Tomás and the Library Lady by Pat Mora

When Jessie Came Across the Sea by Amy Hest

CHAPTER BOOKS

The Arrival by Shaun Tan (wordless graphic novel)

The Boy in the Striped Pajamas by John Boyne

Esperanza Rising by Pam Muñoz Ryan

Harbor Me by Jacqueline Woodson

Hidden Figures, Young Readers' Edition, by Margot Lee Shetterly

Home of the Brave by Katherine Applegate

Inside Out and Back Again by Thanhha Lai

A Long Walk to Water by Linda Sue Park

Number the Stars by Lois Lowry

Refugee by Alan Gratz

ONLINE ARTICLES AND TEXTS

"Former WWII Refugee Sends Hope in a Box to Young Syrian Boy," Newsela article, https://newsela.com/read/refugee-carepackage/id/15788

"Refugee Crisis," Flocabulary video, https://www.flocabulary.com/unit/week-in-rap-extra-refugee-crisis/

Refugee Text Set from Newsela, https://newsela.com/text-sets/153995

"Rohingya Refugees," News in Levels article, www.newsinlevels.com/products/rohingya-refugees-level-3/

"What Are Refugees?," Wonderopolis article, https://wonderopolis.org/wonder/
what-are-refugees

"Young Migrant Workers Toil in U.S. Fields," *Scholastic* article, www.scholastic.com/
browse/article.jsp?id=5426

ONLINE TEACHER RESOURCES

"Julia Moves to the United States," learning plan from Teaching Tolerance based
on a nonfiction story about the writer Julia Alvarez, www.tolerance.org/
classroom-resources/texts/julia-moves-to-the-united-states

"Who Is an Immigrant?," lesson plan from Teaching Tolerance, www.tolerance.org/
classroom-resources/tolerance-lessons/who-is-an-immigrant

CHAPTER 5

Advocating for Change

Be the change that you wish to see in the world.

— Mahatma Gandhi

Never doubt that a small group of thoughtful, committed citizens can change the world; indeed, it's the only thing that ever has.

—Margaret Mead

There are those who say, "Just ignore it and keep going. It isn't our problem." There are those who say, "I'm not getting involved. What can one person do, anyway? What's the point?" Then there are those who can't, for some reason, ignore injustice and hatred and the mistreatment of others. They can't see a wrong and walk away. They believe that one person can make a difference, and they do. What is that special something that drives some of us into action, that fuels us to get involved and work to facilitate change in the world? Apathy is an easy leader to follow, especially when your own life, your own way of being, is not threatened. Our experience has shown us that children see injustice more easily and more clearly than many adults do. Children are more likely to become incensed by conditions that they deem "not fair." Children believe they can make a difference in this big wide world. And we believe in children.

In this chapter, we outline how to reframe the reading and writing workshop with intentional text selection and conversations focused around advocating for change. We believe the topic "advocating for change" demonstrates the power in taking a stand on issues that are important to you. At the end of the chapter, you'll find a list of suggested children's literature focused on a range of topics including, but not limited to, segregation, voting rights, and child labor. Each text offers situations that encourage readers to consider ways the characters question and confront injustice while they become advocates for change. We describe one classroom teacher's journey to help her students think critically about the text, the world, and their role in the world. Join us on this journey as fourth-grade teacher Alyssa Cameron and her students from Roebuck Elementary in Roebuck, South Carolina, discover the power in their own words and actions as they demonstrate that change can begin with one class or one person.

TAKE A MOMENT TO REFLECT

Before you read about Alyssa's journey, think about your class, school, or community. What issues feel particularly relevant and important right now? Maybe you've heard kids talk about or make sense of a recent event in the news. Maybe they are worried for their safety. Maybe they are concerned about their family's immigration status. Whatever the issue, don't feel like you have to be an expert or have all the answers. Just like Alyssa, you are on a learning journey with your students. ■

Voices from the Classroom

Alyssa Cameron continuously strives to build a classroom community with her fourth graders. On the first day of school, her students created a classroom constitution documenting ways they wanted to be treated and how they would treat each other. A clear consensus was established for a classroom community where everyone felt included, respected, and valued.

Selection

Over the course of the year, Alyssa's class read many texts, including picture books, chapter books, poems, articles, and online resources. They read in a variety of settings, including whole-group read-aloud, independent self-selected reading, and student-led book clubs. In each of these settings, she intentionally selected books based on a range of topics and issues that students had expressed interest in. For example, in the fall, when one student shared about his friend at church who had autism, Alyssa recommended books like *Rules* by Cynthia Lord and *Out of My Mind* by Sharon M. Draper to help him better understand life with special needs from different perspectives. During the presidential election as the country became more polarized, Alyssa created a safe environment for her students to examine their differences as well as the similarities that unite them as human beings. They shared belief statements such as "everyone should be treated with kindness" and "everyone should be respected for their differences." This conversation was the foundation for later critical conversations, including powerful discussions when reading the book *Separate Is Never Equal: Sylvia Mendez and Her Family's Fight for Desegregation* by Duncan Tonatiuh.

Alyssa chose *Separate Is Never Equal* after the class engaged in a number of conversations related to racial discrimination. Throughout these conversations, Alyssa noticed that students held the belief that discrimination occurred only between white people and African Americans. Because she wanted to deepen their understandings and assumptions, she selected this book to expand students' awareness and thinking about discrimination against Mexican Americans. This true story is about Sylvia Mendez, a Mexican American who was turned away from a "white only" school and sent to attend a nearby Mexican school. Despite many setbacks, her family successfully fought for the desegregation of schools in California and paved the way for the *Brown v. Board of Education* case that led to desegregation of schools in the United States. Alyssa's class read about Sylvia Mendez and took action to teach others about the important advocacy work of the Mendez family.

Connection

When she introduced the book to the class, Alyssa read the title, showed the cover of the book, and asked students what they noticed and what they were thinking. One child instantly commented, "The black people and the white people are separated." Due to limited prior knowledge, her students made the assumption that the people experiencing segregation were African American. Not until the book stated that Sylvia's family was Mexican American did the students realize the characters were not African American.

Alyssa's students were dismayed with the treatment of Sylvia's family and declared it unfair. "Why are they treated differently because of the way they look? Why didn't they have equal rights?"

Some students made personal connections and others made connections to other historical moments. Students recorded their connections on sticky notes and then shared with a partner before sharing with the whole class. See Figures 5–1 and 5–2 to see students as they record reactions and share with a partner. One student shared that his cousin was rejected from a college for being a Muslim and another student, a Mexican American, wondered if her own parents experienced similar segregation as children. Others made connections to the Jim Crow era when African Americans were forced to sit on the back of the bus and drink from separate water fountains. They compared the Mendez family's fight to have Mexican children admitted to all-white schools to Martin Luther King Jr.'s fight for equality.

FIGURE 5–1 Fourth Grader Jots Down Connections to *Separate Is Never Equal*

FIGURE 5–2 Students Turn and Talk to Share Connections About *Separate Is Never Equal*

Reflection

During a second read, Alyssa's students began to peel back layers of misconceptions about segregation. They were initially unaware of the discrimination faced by Mexican Americans and thought school segregation affected only African Americans. They were shocked and declared it unfair that Sylvia Mendez was not allowed to attend the white school. They noticed, however, that her light-skinned cousins were able to attend. This led to further examination of why Sylvia's family was treated differently. They noticed that the principal could not provide any substantial reasons for sending the Mendez family to a different school. The students also inferred that, in the story, white people viewed themselves as superior and more intelligent than the Mexicans. One student asked, "I wonder who decided that black people should have less— bad schools, no money—and white people could be rich." In response, the students examined the notion of colonialism. One student suggested that perhaps since white Europeans founded the country, white people believe it is their country, with no room for new groups of people, whether they came by choice or force. Another student commented that "because it was founded by the white people, they think they can rule over people who come to their country."

CONSIDERATIONS FOR THE **K–2 Classroom**

Younger students may not have the background knowledge to have informed conversations about colonialism or desegregation. Yet, we can still help them consider issues of inequality and ways to advocate for change by taking a stand on an issue they feel is important. For instance, as part of Katie's dissertation research, first graders discussed topics such as bullying on the playground. After reading a collection of texts about bullying, one group of students decided to write, perform, and film a play to teach others how to stand up to a bully. The class also explored more global issues framed around fairness. When one student made a connection between a read-aloud and a friend from his church who is a former Lost Boy, his classmates had little background knowledge about the Lost Boys or the devastation caused by the civil war in South Sudan. To help answer the children's questions, the teacher invited the former Lost Boy to the class to share his story. Upon learning there was no school in his village, the students were inspired to take action to help raise awareness and funds to support his nonprofit to build a school. One group collaboratively wrote a book to teach others about their new friend and his cause and shared it online using VoiceThread (www. voicethread.com) to expand their audience. Then they decided to place coin jars throughout the school and the community along with signs about their cause. After only a few weeks, the class raised enough money for the first layer of cement bricks for the school. Even young children can take a stand on issues that affect their classroom, school, or communities when we make it relevant to their lives and their curiosities.

To read more about Katie's work and the work of other early childhood educators who weave critical literacy practices with technology integration, you may want to read *Technology and Critical Literacy in Early Childhood Education* by Vivian Vasquez and Carol Felderman (2012) and *For a Better World: Reading and Writing for Social Action* by Randy and Katherine Bomer (2001). ▪

Ultimately, reading and discussing *Separate Is Never Equal* led students to question segregation and take action to make others aware of this injustice. Exposure to literature tapped into an existing knowledge base about the civil rights movement in the American South during the 1950s and 1960s. Further conversation and additional texts that Alyssa selected to stretch their knowledge transformed what may have been a mirror into a window exposing the presence of segregation and racism in the United States. This experience nudged students out of a "curricular comfort zone" resulting from their studies of the civil rights movement. In their minds this was history that happened long ago. Somehow, seeing old information through a new window brought into focus an insight they had not considered.

▪ FOR YOUR CLASSROOM

If the text you select is historical fiction or nonfiction, supplement students' knowledge of that historical period with additional information in the form of

- photographs
- primary documents
- articles or newspaper clippings
- passages from books
- online resources
- video clips
- artifacts
- guest speakers. ▪

Action

Reading the book *Separate Is Never Equal* exposed students to the powerful story of how the Mendez family took a stand for social justice. Because Alyssa's students were unfamiliar with Sylvia's story, they felt it was important to share it with others who also may not know it. As one student shared, "We did not know Sylvia's story, but we agree that it is important. We can prevent this from happening again and spread kindness and acceptance if we share her story." They brainstormed a list of audiences that might benefit from learning Sylvia's story and then explored a variety of ways they could share it. They gathered in small groups based on the selected project to discuss how they would meet the needs of specific audiences, keep the story accurate, and include the "so what?" For instance, one group brainstormed their rationale for sharing the story with the school administration. They stated, "This is important to us and it should be important to you because this is your school and there are black, white, and Hispanic people at this school. We need to make sure that everybody is treated right."

One group of students created an informational PowerPoint to present to school administrators. Another group created a reader's theater script using Google Docs. They practiced and performed the script for kindergartners. You can see an excerpt of the script in Figure 5–3. Yet another group wrote a "Who Was?" book about Sylvia Mendez based on the popular "Who Was?" series after researching and learning that at the time there was no "Who Was?" book written about her. This group also wrote to the series' editor requesting that the publisher consider adding a book about Sylvia

Mendez to the collection. Figure 5–4 shows the text of the student letter to the "Who Was?" editor. The group who shared the PowerPoint presentation with the school's administration was met with praise and an opportunity to be heard by those in power. When the administration (principal, assistant principal, literacy coach, and school officer) asked how they could help, students responded with the need for bulletin board displays and more diverse books in the school's library.

Kyra: Mom, Narrator, Sylvia, School Principal

Josh: Dad, Brothers

Claudia: Cousins, Girl in the Hall, County Director

NARRATOR: This is the true story of Sylvia Mendez and her family's fight for desegregation.

GIRL IN THE HALL: Go back to the Mexican school. You don't belong here!!!!!!!!

SYLVIA: I don't want to go to that school anymore.

MOM: *No sabes que por luchamos.* Don't you know that is why we fought?

NARRATOR: Three years earlier in the summer of 1944, the Mendez family moved from the city of Santa Ana, California, to a farm in nearby Westminster.

MOM: I am here to enroll the children in school.

COUNTY DIRECTOR: They cannot attend this school. They must go to the Mexican school.

SYLVIA: Why do I have to go to the Mexican school? I am not Mexican. I am American. I speak English. My father is from Mexico, but he became a U.S. citizen, and my mother is from Puerto Rico, which is a U.S. territory.

MOM: Is it because we have brown skin and thick black hair and our last name is Mendez?

COUNTY DIRECTOR: Rules are rules. The Mendez children have to go to the Mexican school.

MOM: Then I will not be enrolling them.

DAD: The public school on 17th Street is the closest school to our home. My children should be allowed to attend it.

COUNTY DIRECTOR: Your children have to go to the Mexican school.

DAD: But why? No one will give me a good answer.

FIGURE 5–3 Excerpt of Reader's Theater Script

Dear Editor,

My class and I are huge "Who Was?" fans. I love the "Who Was?" Martin Luther King Jr. book because I like how he used words to fight for rights. In our class, my teacher Miss Cameron read us a book called *Separate Is Never Equal*. It is about a Mexican American girl and her brother who are not allowed to go to a public school and she and her family fight for rights. The girl's name is Sylvia Mendez. I think you should write a "Who Was?" Sylvia Mendez book, because the book could inspire kids across the world to fight for what they believe in. Sylvia is very similar to Martin Luther King because they fought for what they believe in.

FIGURE 5–4 **Student Letter to "Who Was?" Editor**

Separate Is Never Equal broadened students' worldviews to deepen their understanding that segregation and discrimination exist for minority groups other than African Americans, and it gave them the necessary foundational understanding to begin to advocate for change.

Next Steps

Alyssa initiated book clubs to continue to engage students in responsive and critical thinking. Book clubs created a more inclusive atmosphere where all students, including those who may be more reluctant to share in the whole-class setting, felt comfortable discussing their ideas about the text in small peer groups. Alyssa wanted to include books that had characters similar in age to her students. Alyssa also grouped students based on their levels of understanding of diverse experiences and situations. Some students had exhibited empathy and compassion for certain issues but needed to push deeper in conversations. Others were not as familiar with particular issues or needed to challenge themselves to consider alternate perspectives. After selecting books and forming book club groups, the class collaboratively brainstormed and established common goals in a book club contract. You can see a sample book club contract in Figure 5–5.

Book Club Contract

① Everyone needs to agree on page daily goals

② Respect each other's opinions and ideas

③ Stay on task

④ Everyone should get a chance to talk

⑤ Be honest!

⑥ Encourage and support

FIGURE 5–5 **Book Club Contract**

The book clubs provided students with more opportunities to share their thoughts. In a smaller group setting, students had a safer space to introduce new issues related to refugees, migrant workers, and people with special needs. They also continued their conversations about racism. Students traced themes within and across books to ultimately come to some conclusions about social justice using the following questions as a guide.

- Why do we treat people differently?
- How do people respond to difficult topics?
- How do I view the world?
- What can I do myself to promote all people in my individual world?

Alyssa also provided a variety of guiding questions for students to consider while reading:

- How are you like the character?
- How are you different from the character?
- What don't you understand about the character?

Students responded in their journals before their book clubs met. They considered questions like

- What do we know?
- What don't we know?
- What do we need to know?
- What do we think about the main character and the setting?

In addition to learning the necessary literacy skills to meet fourth-grade standards, students were introduced to scenarios in books that made them think about themselves and the world around them. The book clubs sparked meaningful conversations about the issues and how to take action. Some groups set out to learn more about the issues related to the characters in their books. For instance, the group reading *A Long Walk to Water* by Linda Sue Park researched refugees and the group reading *El Deafo* by Cece Bell researched cochlear implants. After reading a variety of sources on their topics, the groups created infographics to share with their peers. See Figures 5–6 and 5–7 for examples of student infographics.

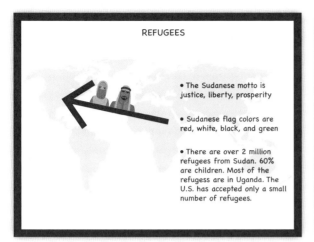

FIGURE 5–6 Student-Created Infographic About Refugees from Sudan Based on *A Long Walk to Water*

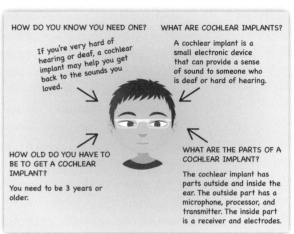

FIGURE 5–7 Student-Created Infographic About Cochlear Implants Based on *El Deafo*

ALTERNATE GRADE EXAMPLE
Fifth Grade

Ngoc, a fifth grader in Morgan Mason's class at Brook Glenn Elementary in Taylors, South Carolina, moved from South Vietnam during second grade. Her family speaks only Vietnamese at home, but Ngoc speaks both Vietnamese and English. She is highly motivated but is very shy and rarely participates in class. When she does speak her volume is nearly inaudible, making it difficult for others to understand what she is saying.

With Ngoc's shy personality, annotations and written summaries of text provided her teacher with a window into her thinking as a reader. With continued scaffolding, Ngoc's annotations moved beyond restating the text to asking questions to dig deeper into the text's meaning. To enhance her reading experience and provide her with low-stakes opportunities to practice oral language skills, Ngoc's teacher partnered her with Abby, one of her peers, to read and discuss texts. Together, the girls read "Malala the Powerful" from Scholastic's *Storyworks* magazine and Abby posed several thoughtful questions that sparked discussion about girls' right to education.

Although Ngoc did not ask many questions herself, she began asking questions about the meaning of unknown words such as *banned*, which was in one of the sub-headings in the article about Malala Yousafzai. She annotated in the margins that the word meant "not allowed." Later she circled the word *defy* and then jotted "break the rules" next to it. During a reading conference, Morgan asked Ngoc how Malala's father defied the Taliban, to ensure her understanding of the vocabulary through application. Ngoc explained that Malala's father continued to run his school after he was told to shut it down.

Ngoc and Abby were excited to find a book on Epic (an online resource made available to students) about how Malala met with President Obama to share her story of advocacy. Then they read the two-voice poem "I Heard It on the Bus One Day" by Jeff Sapp. This poem is told from the perspectives of Rosa Parks and the bus driver. Each girl selected either Rosa Parks or the bus driver and alternated reading the lines, with the bolded lines read in unison. Ngoc and Abby discussed how the poet used specific word choices to convey the characters' emotions, experiences, and perspectives. To help with fluency in Ngoc's reading, Morgan selected a reader's theater script titled "The Day Mrs. Parks Was Arrested." The girls chose roles and practiced their reading over multiple days. They made the Venn diagram shown in Figure 5–8 to compare Malala and Rosa Parks.

Using the information from their Venn diagram, Ngoc and Abby composed their own two-voice poem, modeling it on the one read earlier in the week. The girls sought additional information about Malala and Rosa Parks to incorporate into their poem. Figure 5–9 shows the girls at work, and Figure 5–10 is their two-voice poem. You can see how they divided their poem into three sections—Malala on the left, Rosa Parks on the right, and their similarities in the middle.

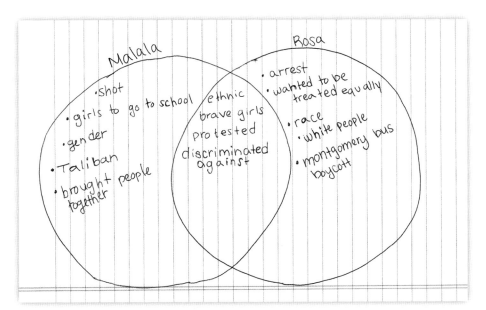

FIGURE 5–8 Venn Diagram to Compare Malala and Rosa Parks

FIGURE 5–9 Ngoc and Abby Writing

FIGURE 5–10 Ngoc and Abby's Two-Voice Poem

Malala Yousafzai	BOTH	Rosa Parks
	Who are we? We are brave girls.	
I stood up for girls' rights to education.		
		I stood up for equal rights for all people.
	We fought for people who were scared to fight for themselves.	
Too scared of the Taliban.		
		Too scared of white people.
	They threatened us.	
I was shot by the Taliban.		
		I was arrested by white policemen.
	Because we broke the rules. People joined us to protest.	
For girls to go to school.		
		To end segregation.
	We were discriminated against. Both of us were banned but we defied those who tried to stop us.	
I continued to go to school.		
		I stayed seated in the front of the bus.
	WE CHANGED HISTORY!	

Suggested Resources

PICTURE BOOKS

Alia's Mission: Saving the Books of Iraq by Mark Alan Stamaty

The Banana-Leaf Ball: How Play Can Change the World by Katie Smith Milway

Beatrice's Goat by Page McBrier

Biblioburro: A True Story from Colombia by Jeanette Winter

The Boy Who Harnessed the Wind by William Kamkwamba and Bryan Mealer

Brave Girl: Clara and the Shirtwaist Makers' Strike of 1909 by Michelle Markel

Coolies by Yin

Drum Dream Girl by Margarita Engle

El Deafo by Cece Bell

Follow the Moon Home: A Tale of One Idea, Twenty Kids, and a Hundred Sea Turtles by Philippe Cousteau and Deborah Hopkinson

For the Right to Learn: Malala Yousafzai's Story by Rebecca Langston-George

Freedom Summer by Deborah Wiles

Give a Goat by Jan West Schrock

Grace Hopper: Queen of Computer Code by Laurie Wallmark

Hands Around the Library: Protecting Egypt's Treasured Books by Susan L. Roth and Karen Leggett Abouraya

Harvesting Hope: The Story of Cesar Chavez by Kathleen Krull

Ian's Walk: A Story About Autism by Laurie Lears

The Librarian of Basra: A True Story from Iraq by Jeanette Winter

Lillian's Right to Vote: A Celebration of the Voting Rights Act of 1965 by Jonah Winter

A Long Walk to Water by Linda Sue Park

Luna and Me: The True Story of a Girl Who Lived in a Tree to Save a Forest by Jenny Sue Kostecki-Shaw

Malala: A Brave Girl from Pakistan / Iqbal: A Brave Boy from Pakistan by Jeanette Winter

Malala: Activist for Girls' Education by Raphaële Frier

Malala's Magic Pencil by Malala Yousafzai

Maybe Something Beautiful: How Art Transformed a Neighborhood by F. Isabel Campoy and Theresa Howell

My Brother Charlie by Holly Robinson Peete and Ryan Elizabeth Peete

Nelson Mandela by Kadir Nelson

One Plastic Bag: Isatou Ceesay and the Recycling Women of the Gambia by Miranda Paul

Out of My Mind by Sharon M. Draper

The Red Bicycle: The Extraordinary Story of One Ordinary Bicycle by Jude Isabella

Ron's Big Mission by Rose Blue and Corinne J. Naden

Rosa by Nikki Giovanni

Rules by Cynthia Lord

Seeds of Change by Jen Cullerton Johnson

Separate Is Never Equal: Sylvia Mendez and Her Family's Fight for Desegregation by Duncan Tonatiuh

¡Sí, Se Puede! Yes, We Can! Janitor Strike in L.A. by Diana Cohn

Sit-In: How Four Friends Stood Up by Sitting Down by Andrea Davis Pinkney

Voice of Freedom: Fannie Lou Hamer: Spirit of the Civil Rights Movement by Carole Boston Weatherford

Wangari's Trees of Peace: A True Story from Africa by Jeanette Winter

The Youngest Marcher: The Story of Audrey Faye Hendricks, a Young Civil Rights Activist by Cynthia Levinson

CHAPTER BOOKS

The Breadwinner by Deborah Ellis

El Deafo by Cece Bell

Esperanza Rising by Pam Muñoz Ryan

Flush by Carl Hiaasen

Hoot by Carl Hiaasen

Locomotion by Jacqueline Woodson

A Long Walk to Water by Linda Sue Park

One Crazy Summer by Rita Williams-Garcia

Out of My Mind by Sharon M. Draper

Peace, Locomotion by Jacqueline Woodson

Rules by Cynthia Lord

Stella by Starlight by Sharon M. Draper

Sylvia and Aki by Winifred Conkling

Where the Mountain Meets the Moon by Grace Lin

MISCELLANEOUS

"The Day Mrs. Parks Was Arrested" by Lauren Tarshis

"I Heard It on the Bus One Day" by Jeff Sapp

"Malala the Powerful" from Scholastic's *Storyworks* magazine

CHAPTER 6

Sharing When You Have Little to Give

No one has ever become poor by giving.

—Anne Frank

If you have much, give of your wealth;
if you have little, give of your heart.

—Arabian proverb

You give little when you give of your possessions. It is when you give of yourself that you truly give.

—Kahlil Gibran

When we think of helping others, we often think of tangible things. We think in terms of what we have to give. That may include donations of clothing, books, food, building supplies, medicine, money, and the like. All too seldom do we realize that we can help with our energy and our talents. We can help with our attitudes, our words, our ways of being with others. Giving is not measured by the pound, in numbers, or in dollars; rather, it is measured by the generosity of spirit and by the care and empathy behind the gift. Simply sharing a smile or a kind word can brighten someone's day.

In this chapter, we highlight the work of two third-grade teachers and their students as they explore ways to share even when you have little to give.

Voices from the Classroom

This chapter features Samantha Rochester and Jeanette Montes, two third-grade teachers working at Grove Elementary, a Title I school in Piedmont, South Carolina. They believe in the idea of innate human kindness and wanted to engage their students in an exploration of the topic of sharing when you have little to give. Many of their students come from low-income families and are dependent on free breakfast and lunch provided by the school. In fact, many of these children receive backpacks with food to take home for the weekends. Samantha and Jeanette wanted to position students to see that they are valuable and have much to offer even if they do not have much in terms of financial or material wealth. Together, the teachers brainstormed a collection of books that fit this theme and then selected books they felt were most appropriate for their individual classes. Through a series of read-aloud experiences and open conversations, the teachers asked their students to consider ways they could be generous, kind, and supportive to others in their classrooms, their school, and their community.

Selection

Samantha and Jeanette selected several texts to facilitate conversations around sharing when you have little to give, including *Ada's Violin: The Story of the Recycled Orchestra of Paraguay* by Susan Hood, *Last Stop on Market Street* by Matt de la Peña, *The Rainbow Fish* by Marcus Pfister, *Each Kindness* by Jacqueline Woodson, *Because Amelia Smiled* by David Ezra Stein, *Boxes for Katje* by Candace Fleming, and *Beatrice's Goat* by Page McBrier. Jeanette later added the book *Dear Primo: A Letter to My Cousin* by Duncan Tonatiuh when one student shared how his uncle assisted with relief efforts in Mexico after a recent earthquake. This personal and specific connection with the theme led the class to read several articles about the effects of the earthquake and the book *Earthquake* by Milly Lee.

Connection

Samantha's class connected with Ada, the main character in *Ada's Violin: The Story of the Recycled Orchestra of Paraguay.* The students didn't comment on the differences between her home and theirs. They didn't mention that she lives in the slums of Uruguay. Rather, they noticed that she has friends, just like they do. Even though her home environment is quite different from their own, they noticed their shared humanity. Several students also mentioned the creativity of the person who made the instruments and connected this with their own inventiveness in making things out of ordinary materials (for example, cardboard, paper towel tubes, and aluminum pie plates) they find around their homes. One student commented that she likes to create through writing just like the author of the book.

After hearing the story read aloud, students were eager to learn more about the man who made the instruments out of materials from the landfill. They were particularly curious about how he made those instruments. Yet they were confused by all the trash in the community and quickly empathized with Ada and her community. They asked questions like "Where do they play when there is a landfill filled with trash everywhere?" and "How did Ada live with all of that trash?" One student said, "I would tell kids to respect everybody no matter where they come from."

This last comment held particular meaning for Samantha because treating others with respect regardless of differences is a key tenet of their classroom community. She hopes this idea will become a core principle that will guide her students throughout their lives.

Samantha chose to read additional books to deepen students' connection to the characters and develop empathy. Children's literature provides rich and robust opportunities to delve into situations from a safe distance. Repeated exposure and making connections across texts can scaffold the development of insights children need to reach a level of empathy and action.

This conversation prompted Samantha to read the book *Last Stop on Market Street* next. In this story, CJ and his nana take the bus to a shelter where they serve food to those in need. During the entire bus ride, CJ notices and longs for material items such as a car and an iPod, but his nana helps him find the beauty and value in everyday things. Samantha's class considered how this book served as a mirror for experiences in their own lives. She began by reviewing why it is important for readers to make connections with texts. Students replied with comments such as "I think you understand the characters and stay focused on the characters" and "You might see some of your own actions in the book." Then she asked students, "How does seeing ourselves in books helps us as human beings?" Samantha paused and waited a few seconds before asking them to share their thoughts, then recorded their ideas on an anchor chart. See Figures 6–1a and 6–1b for the anchor charts Samantha created with students' responses.

FIGURE 6–1a (below)
"Books as Mirrors" Anchor Chart

FIGURE 6–1b (right)
"Books as Windows" Anchor Chart

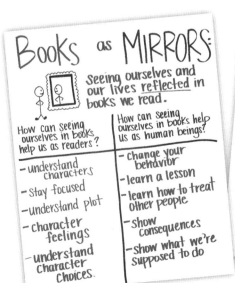

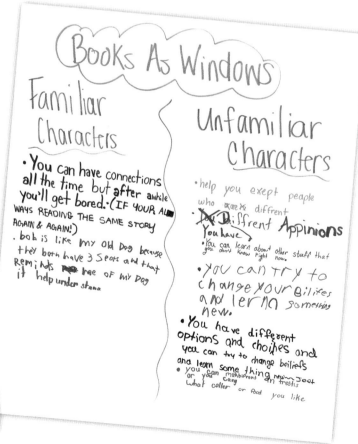

After reading, Samantha shared some of her own connections to the book: "Like CJ, I wasn't that excited when we first decided to go serve food at the soup kitchen on Thanksgiving, and I didn't fully understand the importance of it until afterward. It's like in the story when it said CJ's heart felt full. That is how my heart felt." Students chimed in:

STUDENT: When my mom takes me somewhere, I feel like CJ did in the book. I am not excited about it. It's super boring and I don't like it.

STUDENT: I agree. In the book, when it first started and he left home, he felt freedom and I feel like that when I get out and play. Sometimes I don't get why I am not sorry for anything. Sometimes my brother and I get into arguments and my mom says that we shouldn't have done that.

The students agreed that "CJ learned not to be selfish at the end when they cook and hand out food."

Meanwhile in Jeanette's class, students discussed the book *Beatrice's Goat* and explored the overlapping themes across the collection of books they had been reading. In this story, Beatrice does not have enough money to go to school, but her life changes when she buys a goat. The goat's offspring and milk bring money to Beatrice's family. Students expressed empathy for Beatrice and commented that they are lucky to be able to go to school. They also noticed obvious differences between how people live in different countries, drawing attention to homes and clothing. However, they recognized their common humanity, as revealed by the comment that they "all have caring hearts." They added that it is important to remember "not to be selfish and care for others who may need help."

JEANETTE: Now that we've read these books, how have your thoughts changed?

STUDENT: If I had enough gifts to give away, I would share with my class.

STUDENT: We should share the book with people who don't like to share. When they read it, they will like it and start sharing things.

STUDENT: I can share good thoughts with my younger brother, who will then share it with our other little brother, and we can keep passing it to our family and friends.

JEANETTE: Yes, that is how we can pass it on to the whole world.

STUDENT: If you see someone who ran out of gas, you could stop and help them.

STUDENT: All the people from every state in the United States can help Mexican people. Because some people in Mexico had an earthquake and they don't have no houses or clothes. My uncle is going and we gave him a lot of clothes. My family is there and they are poor.

Students reflected on the theme of giving after reading *Beatrice's Goat*. It led one student to make connections to a recent earthquake in Mexico, where his family is from. He told his peers about how his family is sharing and helping by donating supplies. Jeanette used this as an opportunity to create a more inclusive classroom by tapping into students' funds of knowledge, the knowledge gained from family and cultural backgrounds (Moll et al. 1992).

TAKE A MOMENT TO REFLECT

How does your own teaching practice link student learning to family and culture? Take a moment to write about the practices in your classroom that support students' funds of knowledge. ◼

Many of the students in Jeanette's class have family in Mexico, so she chose the book *Dear Primo: A Letter to My Cousin*. It serves as both a mirror and a window for many of her students. In the story, one cousin, Charlie, lives in the United States and the other, Carlitos, lives in Mexico. They write letters back and forth to share about their lives in their respective homes. For the students who did not have family in Mexico, this book provided them with a window into the character's life in Mexico while also offering a mirror into Charlie's life in the United States. Most students were able to identify with both characters.

Reflection

Before reading aloud, Jeanette asked students if they knew the word *primo*. Some students excitedly replied, "Yes, it's 'cousin' in Spanish!" Next, she explained that they would be reading the book *Dear Primo* and asked students to consider in what ways they are similar to and different from the two cousins, Charlie and Carlitos. As she read aloud, some kids spontaneously chimed in with the reading of the labeled Spanish words in the text (for example, *burro*, *pollos*, and *perros*). Other students noted that they learned new words after reading this book. One child said, "I didn't know Spanish words before." This led to a conversation about how all languages are valued and we can work together to help each other learn new words in different languages. Several students commented that they are most like the character Carlitos because they speak Spanish at home and make Mexican food. Yazmin's written reflection can be seen in Figure 6–2. Like many children in her class and in schools across the United States, she identifies with both her Mexican and American heritage.

> Yazmin
>
> ## Dear Primo
>
> I think I am more like Carlitos because my parents are from mexico. And I am confuesed because I know more english than spanish. I am diffrent from america because in my house I talk spansh but in school I talk english, exept when I am talking with my friends, I love spanish!

FIGURE 6–2 Yazmin's Reflection for *Dear Primo: A Letter to My Cousin*

FOR YOUR CLASSROOM

The use of bilingual texts facilitates inclusive experiences for English learners through exposure to familiar language. These experiences are yet another "mirror" that validates culture, language, and prior knowledge. Additionally, bilingual texts serve as "windows" as they expose English speakers to other languages, expanding vocabularies while enhancing connections with peers who speak other languages. ▪

When students reflected on what they had in common with Carlitos and Charlie, they had an opportunity to think about their multifaceted identities. Several children were born in the United States to Mexican American parents, so many identified with the culture and language in both the United States and Mexico, their parents' home country. As one child said, "I had mariachis at a party at my house once. And I like hip-hop. I like to dance and sing, so I am like both characters."

ISAAC: I am like Carlitos because I like quesadillas with green hot salsa. In Mexico when I went when I was little, I got on a horse. I went to work on some hills with my grandpa because his legs hurt. We picked corn and some beans and we walked back with it and saw chickens and we went to a shop at the market. Sometimes we went to a store and we bought corn to take it back to the house to throw it to the chickens. Sometimes we went to this lady who has a machine that breaks the corn up and made it to tortillas. She puts them in the oven and it's more different. Something else that makes me like Carlitos is when I was at Mexico my grandma boiled hot water and gave me cold water and I went to this little house and I showered there. You know, in Mexico there is like restrooms that are away from the house outside. I always bring my own water to shower. My uncle went to Mexico to help with the earthquake. My mom and dad bought supplies like Band-Aids and alcohol, and she told my uncle to bring it to Mexico City. He's trying to get people out of the earthquake.

Isaac's connection to the story piqued his classmates' interest in the need to help people in Mexico who had suffered from the effects of the recent earthquake. Jeanette capitalized on that interest and invited Ms. Trejo, Isaac's mom, to come to the class and explain how she and others were working together to help the people in Mexico. By positioning Isaac and his family as resources for teaching and learning, Jeanette demonstrates that Isaac's family's language and literacy practices are valued.

TAKE A MOMENT TO REFLECT

Connecting home and school in this way provides authentic learning experiences that help shape the teacher's and students' perception of the parents and the community. Stop and consider how you involve your students' families as resources in their learning. ■

During Ms. Trejo's visit, she asked students what they knew about earthquakes and went on to explain the need to build more stable buildings in Mexico that could withstand future earthquakes. She showed the class photos and a video clip of her brother, Isaac's uncle, who was in Mexico to help with the recovery efforts.

Ms. Trejo explained that the workers wore hard hats for protection and remained as quiet as possible so they could hear calls for help from people who remained trapped under the rubble. She described their system of holding up two fingers or a fist when sounds were heard. Other volunteers worked to remove debris from the fallen buildings. Students were fascinated and wanted to know how they could help.

Ms. Trejo said that she sent supplies like gauze, peroxide, Band-Aids, and flashlights to assist the rescuers. She explained that a store near the school was filling trucks with supplies to send to Mexico. She paused and asked students to consider how they could help even in very small ways.

MS. TREJO: Just like the workers in Mexico, we can do a little bit to help no matter where. Mexico. California. Just to give a little bit. Some of us don't have much, but you give with all your heart. That's what matters. We need to think about what matters in our hearts. What can we give from our heart?

STUDENT: Be kind.

STUDENT: Be respectful.

STUDENT: Donate.

STUDENT: Be polite.

STUDENT: Be inspired to help.

STUDENT: Be a supportive person.

STUDENT: Send cards.

STUDENT: Send clothes and food in a truck.

STUDENT: Pray.

After discussing how they could help, students thanked Ms. Trejo and took a picture with her, as seen in Figure 6–3. They invited her to sign the class social contract. Figures 6–4 shows Ms. Trejo signing the contract, and Figure 6–5 shows the contract. One student explained, "We have a contract to remind us to be kind, be better friends, and to be great listeners and help people."

Every place. Every culture. Every family has stories to share.

—Linda Sue Park

FIGURE 6–3
Ms. Trejo Visits the Class to Share About the Rescue Efforts in Mexico After the Earthquake

FIGURE 6–4 (below, left)
Ms. Trejo Signs the Class Social Contract

FIGURE 6–5 (below, right)
Class Social Contract

Action

After reading and discussing collections of texts organized around the idea of sharing when you have little to give, Samantha's students discussed ideas for launching a kindness campaign. Their ideas are listed in Figure 6–6. They ultimately decided to take action by showing their appreciation for others with notes of gratitude and handmade gifts. See Figure 6–7 for an image of the class with their notes and gifts and Figure 6–8 for one student's gratitude note. Each child thought about a person at the school who had influenced him or her in a positive way and hand delivered his or her note and gift to that individual. Students brightened many people's days when they surprised them with a special delivery, as seen in Figures 6–9a and 6–9b.

KINDNESS CAMPAIGN PROJECT IDEAS

Miss Rochester's Class—Third Grade

- Write thank-you notes to custodians
- Help custodians clean the cafeteria after lunch
- Create a book for the principal
- Write thank-you letters to second-grade teachers
- Help the cafeteria serve food
- Bring flowers to the ladies in the office
- Deliver a chocolate bar to each teacher
- Help clean the office
- Deliver small gifts to adults in the building
- Introduce new students to our school
- Pick up playground trash
- Read to a kindergartner
- Tutor a kindergarten class
- Take out the trash for related arts teachers
- Help custodians take out the trash
- Decorate the school for Christmas
- Make ornaments for teachers
- Bake cookies for teachers in school
- Pick up jackets left on the playground to put in the lost and found
- Write a thank-you card for the nurse

FIGURE 6–6 Kindness Campaign Brainstorming

FIGURE 6–7 **Samantha's Class with Their Gratitude Notes**

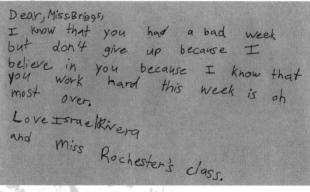

Dear, Miss.Briggs,
I know that you had a bad week
but don't give up because I
believe in you because I know that
you work hard this week is oh
most over.
Love Israel Rivera
and miss Rochester's class.

FIGURE 6–8 (above)
Israel's Gratitude Note

FIGURES 6–9a and
6–9b (left)
Sharing Gratitude
Notes and Flowers
with School Staff

Dear Ashton,

Thank you so much for your kind letter! It surely made me smile! ☺ Keep spreading kindness around the school. With your help, we can make the world a better place!

♡ Mrs. Rodgers

FIGURE 6–10 Mrs. Rodgers' Response to Ashton

One student reflected on the experience after delivering the handmade card: "For my kindness project, I made a card for Mrs. Evans and she felt amazing." Another student, Ashton, reported, "When we were making a letter and I delivered it to Mrs. Rodgers, it made me happy. And after the fire drill, Mrs. Rodgers gave me a letter and it made me feel really good." Mrs. Rodgers' note is in Figure 6–10.

Other students shared similar sentiments: "I feel good about myself by making others feel good about themselves." "I wrote a note to a teacher and I felt so happy because I never did that in my whole life. I was thankful and I loved when she told me to come to her office and she showed me what I made her and she hung it on the wall so she can smile every time she sees it."

The students also created a class book to give the school principal. Figures 6–11a and 6–11b show two pages from the thank-you book.

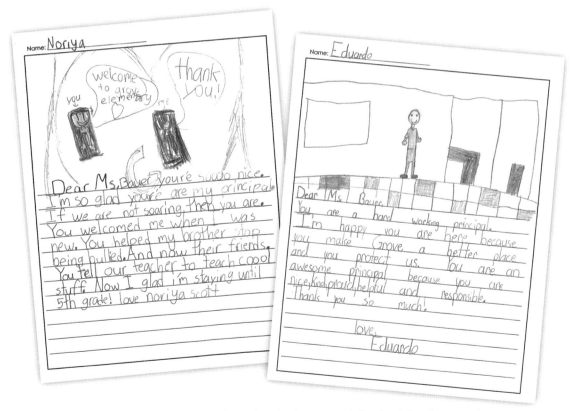

FIGURES 6–11a and 6–11b Two Pages from the Thank-You Book for the School Principal

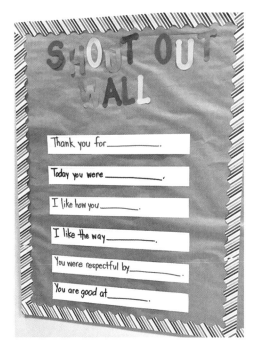

FIGURE 6–12 Jeanette's Class Shout-Out Wall

After reading and talking about the collection of books, Jeanette's students reflected on how to help others in need even when you don't have much to give. They brainstormed ways to help others by giving things like food, supplies, money, and clothing. They decided they could also share their energy and talents (volunteering, being caring, being generous, inspiring people, and simply loving others). Ultimately, they decided to share their love of books with younger children in their school. Their class partnered with a kindergarten class as reading buddies. The experience inspired them to want to show growth in their reading to help beginning readers. This partnership extended throughout the remainder of the year. They also decided to create a shout-out wall where they could share their appreciation for their peers all year long. An image of the shout-out wall is in Figure 6–12.

Next Steps

When they returned from winter break, Jeanette's class reviewed their readings, discussions, and actions regarding sharing when you have little to give. Jeanette read aloud an article about a local girl named Adahlia who gave back to the community in a project called "For Frankie" (www.forfrankie.org/). Each week, Frankie came to the thrift store where Adahlia worked to buy an outfit to replace the previous outfit that was dirty and discarded. Sometimes people have to consider whether to spend money on food that day or on money to wash their clothes. So Adahlia decided to help Frankie do her laundry. Every Wednesday she washes people's clothes for free. She reached out to the community for support and to raise money. At the laundromat, she spends time talking to people and playing games with the children. Oftentimes, community members bring food to share as a way of saying thank you.

Before reading this article, Jeanette knew she had to determine students' prior knowledge of and experiences in laundromats to guide the discussion. Jeanette soon discovered that a few of her students were familiar with the laundromats in the area. While Jeanette was reading, one student commented, "It's boring. That's why kids bring toys to play with." Another said, "I feel so happy for them because when I go to the laundromat, I see kids there just sitting down playing on their mom's phone." These comments reflect some students' prior knowledge of experiences at the laundromat.

JEANETTE: This story in the news is an example of how we can donate our time and our heart when we don't have material items to share.

STUDENT: To have to decide to eat or do laundry is a little sad. The part that I'm glad about is that she is nice to them and does stuff with them and helps them do their laundry.

JEANETTE: All year we have been talking about helping others in the community, in other countries, and in the same city. Let's not forget that we can help others in the community even if we don't have much to give.

STUDENT: I helped my aunt make dessert for my family.

STUDENT: I gave out gloves to people in New York. There's a lot of snow there. We gave them to people that were sitting down on the street that were homeless. They were excited and said thank you.

STUDENT: We were having Christmas dinner and we had to go to the store. I saw a guy who almost fell on the ice and I helped him across the street.

STUDENT: I helped my mom make Christmas presents and wrap presents and do the tree. My grandma was at my house. I helped her get down from the steps because she wasn't feeling good and her heart isn't good.

Notice how Jeanette maintained a focus on the theme that had guided the students' work before the holiday break. By bringing in an article from the local news featuring a person in need, Jeanette made the issue local, relevant, and personal. This conversation reveals that students continued to reflect on the work they had done prior to the break. Jeannette's students were making connections within and across texts to deepen their understanding of how people can give back. This suggests that her students were beginning to fold these ideas into their way of being.

ALTERNATE EXAMPLE
A Different Third-Grade Classroom

Students in Suzie Schmalbeck's third-grade class at Grove Elementary in Piedmont, South Carolina, were already familiar with Shel Silverstein's book *The Giving Tree*. As she read, Suzie asked students to consider how it helps us as readers to see ourselves in the books we read. One child pointed out, "It helps us keep our minds straight." But when the teacher asked the students to consider how a book can serve as a window that lets us see into another way of thinking about something or someone, one student commented that in the case of *The Giving Tree*, he paid more attention to the tree's feelings than those of the boy. Although the story is positioned to influence the reader to see the tree as kind, generous, and giving, as suggested by the title, Suzie's students directed their attention to the boy. Was he kind, generous, and giving? Or was he selfish for constantly taking from the tree?

This conversation led to a discussion about how trees provide us with resources such as money, paper, houses, and even shade. But what happens when the trees keep getting cut down? This conversation led Suzie to read *The Great Kapok Tree: A Tale of the Amazon Rain Forest* by Lynne Cherry and *Ada's Violin: The Story of the Recycled Orchestra of Paraguay* by Susan Hood. Returning to the metaphor of books as windows, Suzie's students explored how reading changed them. One student observed, "You can change. If you are reading a book and you feel how the character feels, you can change." They were inspired by Ada's story. "She didn't have a lot of money," a student commented. "She was sad because a violin could cost more than a house where she lived. She wanted to play. So they made a violin and other instruments out of trash. Now she's a big hit and travels all over the world just to play for people." The conversation eventually shifted to the need to recycle. Suzie's students took action and began a recycling club at their school. The proud members of the recycling club can be seen in Figure 6–13.

FIGURE 6–13 Third-Grade Recycling Club

Suggested Resources

PICTURE BOOKS

Ada's Violin: The Story of the Recycled Orchestra of Paraguay by Susan Hood

Beatrice's Goat by Page McBrier

Because Amelia Smiled by David Ezra Stein

Boxes for Katje by Candace Fleming

A Chair for My Mother by Vera B. Williams

Dear Primo: A Letter to My Cousin by Duncan Tonatiuh

Each Kindness by Jacqueline Woodson

Earthquake by Milly Lee

Four Feet, Two Sandals by Karen Lynn Williams and Khadra Mohammed

14 Cows for America by Carmen Agra Deedy

Give a Goat by Jan West Schrock

The Giving Tree by Shel Silverstein

The Great Kapok Tree: A Tale of the Amazon Rain Forest by Lynne Cherry

Last Stop on Market Street by Matt de la Peña

Maddi's Fridge by Lois Brandt

Mama Panya's Pancakes: A Village Tale from Kenya by Mary Chamberlin and Rich Chamberlin

One by Kathryn Otoshi

One Hen by Katie Smith Milway

An Orange for Frankie by Patricia Polacco

Ordinary Mary's Extraordinary Deed by Emily Pearson

The Rainbow Fish by Marcus Pfister

Rechenka's Eggs by Patricia Polacco

Ruth and the Green Book by Calvin Alexander Ramsey and Gwen Strauss

A Sick Day for Amos McGee by Philip C. Stead

The Teddy Bear by David McPhail

Those Shoes by Maribeth Boelts

CHAPTER BOOKS

Among the Hidden by Margaret Peterson Haddix

Belle Teal by Ann M. Martin

The Breadwinner by Deborah Ellis

Rickshaw Girl by Mitali Perkins

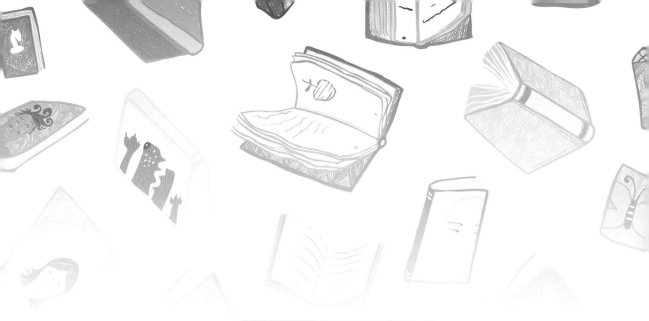

CHAPTER 7

Honoring Others

As human beings, our job in life is to help people realize how rare and valuable each one of us really is, that each of us has something that no one else has—or ever will have—something inside that is unique to all time. It's our job to encourage each other to discover that uniqueness and to provide ways of developing its expression.

—Fred Rogers

The greatest gift that you can give to others is the gift of unconditional love and acceptance.

—Brian Tracy

READING TO MAKE A DIFFERENCE **ONLINE RESOURCES**
To access the online videos for *Reading to Make a Difference,* either scan this QR code or visit
http://hein.pub/ReadingToMakeADifference-login. Enter your email address and password
(or click "Create New Account" to set up an account). Once you have logged in, enter keycode
SPEAKFREE and click "Register."

Stand back and watch a group of very young children at play. More often than not, they are eager to play with everyone without regard for any differences between them. Young children may well be the most accepting humans on the earth. It is the adults in their lives who begin to build walls of division with the bricks of difference. Children learn from adults that some differences are valued while others are seen as a deficit, a reason to step back and get distance from another person. Think about your own upbringing. Which differences in this list were the valued ones?

- tall, short
- thin, heavy
- blonde hair, brown hair, black hair, red hair, straight hair, curly hair, coarse hair, thin hair, long hair, short hair, cornrows, ponytails, pigtails
- green eyes, brown eyes, blue eyes, hazel eyes, amber eyes, "four eyes"
- old clothes, trendy new clothes, clothes that fit well, hand-me-downs
- athletic, artistic, quiet, talkative
- rural life, town life, city life
- house, condo, apartment, trailer
- car riders, bus riders, walkers, bike riders

Chances are you can look back into your own childhood and recall the value assigned (positive or negative) to each trait or circumstance. It is likely that you could easily add to the list. Cultural norms and adult attitudes and behaviors define for children which differences matter and which do not. By the time children reach school age, most have adopted the attitudes and behaviors modeled in their homes and communities. Usually those attitudes and behaviors manifest at school—in the classroom, on the playground, and in the lunchroom.

Even very young children are aware that many people view differences as an opportunity to exclude, embarrass, or shame another individual. This reminds us of the story a friend told about her nephew. At the time, he was a kindergartner who expressed angst about the possibility of his little sister getting picked on because she looked different after being diagnosed with a brain tumor. She had lost her hair from chemotherapy and had some developmental delays resulting in her use of a walker. His deep concern for even the potential of these events reveals that we have work to do.

Our classrooms can be a tapestry of friendships woven from the threads of differences that exist in our communities, indeed, from the world at large. This chapter features a collection of texts selected to bring our differences to the forefront, where we can notice them and name them and celebrate them. Through a series of read-aloud experiences and guided conversations, we structure opportunities for children to note how differences exist within the larger human family. We draw attention to the idea that our humanity is what we have in common with all human beings, but our differences are what make each of us interesting in this world.

Voices from the Classroom

Britney Ross is a first-grade teacher at Francine Delany New School for Children in Asheville, North Carolina, where the mission statement proclaims a schoolwide commitment to "promoting social justice and preserving the inherent worth and dignity of every person," as well as "ongoing learning, raising awareness, and fostering conversations around issues of social justice." It was a natural extension of her daily work to delve into a study of a set of books focused on honoring others.

Selection

Britney chose three books to explore this theme: *Each Kindness* by Jacqueline Woodson, *Those Shoes* by Maribeth Boelts, and *Enemy Pie* by Derek Munson. *Each Kindness* provides an opportunity for reflection, the chance to recognize the impact of not taking an opportunity to be kind. *Those Shoes* allows the reader inside the home and thoughts of a student who lives with his grandmother, who reminds him, "There's no room for 'want' around here—just 'need'" (Boelts 2007). *Enemy Pie* makes space for readers to reflect on the notion that friendships are built by getting to know a person. Britney and her class read each book several times, paying careful attention to how characters are included or excluded and how characters change over time.

Connection

Britney began with *Each Kindness* to help students empathize with a character who is left out and ostracized because of the clothes she wears. The students recognized the situation and considered how Maya felt. Their insight was a window into the feelings of many young children.

Britney capitalized on the power of the illustrations in the picture book. She directed students to zoom in on cues provided by the artist. Among the many benefits of picture books is this opportunity to explore layers of meaning in both the language and art. In this way, the art serves as a mirror for some and as a window for others as they see their own feelings reflected or have the opportunity to see into the feelings of someone else. Notice how Britney leads the students to explore the potential mirrors in this text.

BRITNEY: I heard you say that you noticed the narrator moved her desk away and looked out the window. Those are all nonverbal, yet they totally spoke to Maya and told her that she was not welcomed here. Sometimes you don't have to say anything at all and you still communicate things to other people. How do you see yourself in this book?

STUDENT: I wanted to be kind to Maya and I wanted her to have more friends.

STUDENT: I wanted to stand up for Maya.

[Several students agreed.]

STUDENT: I felt sad for Maya. I didn't want her to be treated this way.

BRITNEY: What would you like to tell Chloe or other characters?

STUDENT: If I was in that book, I would tell Chloe not to act like that or don't do that and eventually no one will be her friend.

STUDENT: I would say to Chloe and the others, "Can you please stop being mean. Maya is my friend and I don't like when you do that." I would stand up for her.

When Britney asked her students how they saw themselves in this story, and then asked what they would tell Chloe and the other characters, she provided an opportunity for them to step inside the story. These comments reveal their awareness of exclusion, their insight about how exclusion diminishes others, and their empathy for Maya. An additional, yet important, insight from this exchange is the recognition of the impact of excluding others: a student commented on Chloe's actions, " . . . eventually no one will be her friend."

FOR YOUR CLASSROOM
Guiding Questions

Guiding questions should move beyond lifting text from the page as an answer; they should spark reflection and thought. Here are a few questions that work well for most any story:

- How do you see yourself in this book?
- What would you like to tell [main character] or one of the other characters?
- How did your thoughts or feelings change as we have talked about this book?
- What do you understand now that you had not thought about before?
- How are you different now that we have read this book?
- Who changed the most in this story? Tell more about that.

Reflection

Britney gently guided this conversation in a new direction, toward reflection, with a single question: So, what can we learn from this book?

> STUDENT: We should be kind every single day, every single minute, every single second.

> STUDENT: It only matters what's on the inside.

> BRITNEY: How could we take action? I don't want you to say anything yet; that will be our next step. But remember that each kindness you do ripples out into the world and you may not get another chance. So your mission today and the days after is to start being kind every chance you get. Make choices that are inclusive; make choices that are kind and welcoming; make choices that are not based on what people are wearing, what they have, or what they look like on the outside.

Britney's invitation to reflect ("I don't want you to say anything yet . . .") suggests to her students that she sees reading as an active process. It suggests that she understands that the impact of a story lingers in the mind of the reader long after the book is closed. It suggests that what we make of a story, how we are moved and possibly changed by a story, comes in layers and over time. She is modeling the power of revisiting a story in your mind.

Britney continued the study with *Those Shoes* and *Enemy Pie*. Each of these stories provides a slightly different angle for considering the impact of inclusion and exclusion. She and her students reflected on what they noticed across the three books and constructed the chart in Figure 7–1 to record their insights. Note the similarity in their comments in the "So What?" column.

BOOK	CHARACTERS	DESCRIPTION	CHARACTER CHANGES	COMPARE/ CONTRAST	MESSAGE / "SO WHAT?"
Each Kindness	Maya Chloe	A girl moved to a new school. She dressed differently and ate different foods because she couldn't afford more, and the kids in her new school mistreated her. They were exclusive and did not invite her in to play with them and always said no when she asked them to play with her. Finally, Maya moved to a different school.	Chloe changed when she participated in the classroom challenge to drop a rock in the bucket for kindness. She realized that she hadn't been nice or kind and was unable to drop her rock in the bucket. She wanted so badly for Maya to come back–for a moment when she could be kind to Maya–but it never happened.	This is the first book read, so there is nothing to compare or contrast it with yet.	You don't always get a second chance. Be kind the first time. It doesn't matter what is on the outside–it matters how you treat people and how you act on the inside.

FIGURE 7–1 **Book Comparison Chart**

(continues)

BOOK	CHARACTERS	DESCRIPTION	CHARACTER CHANGES	COMPARE/ CONTRAST	MESSAGE / "SO WHAT?"
Those Shoes	Jeremy Antonio	Jeremy wanted a new pair of shoes because he thought they would make him fast and he wanted to stay the fastest. Plus, everyone had those shoes. He was able to get a pair of shoes, but they were too small.	Jeremy changed when he decided that Antonio needed those shoes more than he did. He decided to give them to Antonio, who was the only person who did not make fun of or laugh at Jeremy's shoes, which he had to get from the guidance counselor.	Just like Maya, Jeremy felt judged or was excluded because of things on the outside (how he dressed and what he could or could not afford).	What you want and need are two different things sometimes. Be your own person. It doesn't matter what is on the outside–it matters how you treat people and how you act on the inside. People remember how you make them feel.
Enemy Pie	Jeremy Ross Narrator–boy	The boy thought that Jeremy Ross was exclusive. Jeremy didn't invite the boy to his birthday and laughed at him on the baseball field. So the boy was going to make an "enemy pie" to get back at him.	The boy changed when he invited Jeremy Ross to play because he wanted to share some of his enemy pie but ended up having fun with Jeremy.	The boy felt excluded like Maya and Jeremy (*Those Shoes*). Exclusion does not feel good.	Treat people with kindness–include them, ask them to play, and get to know them.

FIGURE 7–1 Book Comparison Chart (*continued*)

Britney and her students returned to *Each Kindness* to discuss their reflections and consider how they are different for having explored these three books. Their conversation led to the decision to do something, to take action to remind others that kindness matters.

Students were not just empathizing with a character, but going deeper, exploring how they can change their own behavior to make sure that no one in their sphere will feel like the characters in these books. Britney nudged the students toward some tangible and manageable action: "So, I want us to start thinking about taking action within our classroom, our school community, and our local community and about how we can start changing the world for the better."

BRITNEY: How are you changed or how do you feel differently now that we have read *Each Kindness*?

STUDENT: It made me want to jump into that book and stand up for Maya and tell everyone it doesn't matter what she looks like or what she eats. We should just be nice!

STUDENT: Sometimes we don't get another chance, so we should be kind the first time and every chance that you get.

STUDENT: It makes me want to look for people in our classroom who may feel excluded. Or maybe at recess or snack-and-wiggle, if I see someone playing on their own, I could go ask if they want to play with me so that they feel more included.

STUDENT: Now that we've read this book, I could go get a trusted adult when I see children that are being excluded.

A LOOK INTO
THE CLASSROOM

Sit in on a discussion and join Jessica, a second-grade teacher, and her students at Francine Delany New School in Asheville, North Carolina, as they revisit and discuss the theme of honoring others in *The Invisible Boy* by Trudy Ludwig.

Action

Britney's class' conversation resulted in three suggestions:

1. Start a kindness project and do an act of kindness a day.
2. Make a video of kindness and send it out to the school.
3. Make posters about being kind and post them around school and our town.

The students reflected and revisited their ideas and then voted to select a class project. The poster project won. Britney and her first graders made thoughtful posters to encourage and promote kindness. The posters were laminated and hung around the school campus and in the community beyond the school. In Figure 7–2 you can see Britney and her class holding up the signs they made. Figure 7–3 shows one of the signs close up, and in Figure 7–4 you can see Britney and some of her students hanging up one of the signs in the community.

FIGURE 7–2 (top) Britney and Her Class Hold Up Kindness Posters

FIGURE 7–3 (bottom, left) Examples of Kindness Posters

FIGURE 7–4 (bottom, right) Britney and Her Students Hang Kindness Posters in the Community

Next Steps

Much to their surprise, Britney's students received a letter from a local community member. In the letter, their neighbor explained how much she appreciated the signs they hung in the community. She told them that one day she was feeling sad, but when she saw their signs she felt much love and that the signs gave her heart the boost it needed to take care of what was making her sad. This powerful example demonstrated for these young children that they too could make a difference in the lives of others.

The letter from the neighbor reignited the students' commitment to spreading kindness. Britney's class made a promise to look for opportunities to be kind and helpful in school and in the community.

ALTERNATE GRADE EXAMPLE
Fifth Grade

Reading aloud *Wonder* by R. J. Palacio provided a strong foundation for Susan Bukowski's fifth-grade students at Pine Lake Preparatory School in Mooresville, North Carolina, as they dove into the theme of accepting others. Students made connections within and across texts. For instance, when they read *Lailah's Lunchbox: A Ramadan Story* by Reem Faruqi, one student commented that Lailah had trouble being accepted, just like August, but for different reasons. This child made connections about acceptance and how we perceive other students who may appear different from ourselves.

Susan then read *One Green Apple* by Eve Bunting and students discussed the theme and shared their thinking and personal connections:

> STUDENT: [I felt left out and alone like the character] when everyone was doing one thing and I was doing another or I was behind and because I am the only Indian in this class.

> STUDENT: One time I didn't choose to be kind–I was at a football game. After a play, someone pushed me and I threw him to the ground.

STUDENT: I felt lost at school when I didn't know what to do when my dog died and I didn't want to tell anyone.

STUDENT: In the story, Farah states that she felt "lost." I have felt lost sometimes. One of the times was when my mom told me I would get a little brother. I was both excited and confused.

STUDENT: I've been scared at school before. When it was my first day here, I was speechless and nervous!

Susan appreciated how her students shared ideas and personal experiences. She commented, "I would like to have students share a little bit about their own cultures and backgrounds. I'm not sure how that will look yet, but this is one of the ideas that many students said they want to do because of reading the books. I think it's a great idea! I'm so happy that the students want to share and learn more about each other."

After reading books such as *Wonder, Lailah's Lunchbox, One Green Apple*, and *Angel Child, Dragon Child* by Michele Maria Surat and analyzing the characters, plot, theme, and relevance to their own lives, Susan's students explored the books' significance and why their messages matter.

Susan's students recorded ways to choose to be kind on sticky notes. When Andrew suggested a buddy bench to create a change on the playground, the entire class quickly agreed. You can see Andrew's sticky note in Figure 7–5. He said, "During recess, I see kids standing alone or just by themselves, and I know there are a lot of people on the playground who would want to play with them if they knew they were alone. . . . That's when I thought of the buddy bench, where kids can go to it, and other kids can see them and talk to them and be friends with them" (quoted in Ghani 2018). Andrew knew firsthand what it felt like to make new friends as he had already been to five different schools. His experience provided a mirror for him to empathize with the children on the playground and led him to spring into action along with the help of his classmates, teacher, and school community.

3. The 5th Grade at Pine Lake Prep can create a buddy bench, for the lonly kids at recess.

Andrew

FIGURE 7–5 Andrew's Sticky Note Suggestion to Create a Buddy Bench

After much discussion, the students decided to create a buddy bench for the playground. There were three benches on school property not being used due to their location behind the athletic center. Two of the three benches literally faced a brick wall. The students decided that the three benches should be moved to the playground and two of the benches should be transformed to buddy benches. They elicited help from the parents to refinish and repaint the benches and raised money through a penny war campaign in which they collected pocket change. They visited other classrooms to inform them of the purpose of the buddy bench and read the book *The Mystery at Palace Street School* by Sandy Mahony and Mary Lou Brown. The buddy bench was revealed to the entire school with a ribbon-cutting ceremony and a balloon release with a reminder to choose to be kind. Students can be seen gathering and releasing balloons at the buddy bench ribbon-cutting ceremony in Figures 7–6a and 7–6b.

FIGURE 7–6a
(left) Students Gathered for the Buddy Bench Ceremony

FIGURE 7–6b
(below) Balloons Released During the Buddy Bench Ceremony

If you have a choice between being right and being kind, choose kind.

—Dr. Wayne W. Dyer

Suggested Resources

PICTURE BOOKS

And Tango Makes Three by Justin Richardson and Peter Parnell

Angel Child, Dragon Child by Michele Maria Surat

Baseball Saved Us by Ken Mochizuki

Big Red Lollipop by Rukhsana Khan

Blue Skies for Lupe by Linda Kurtz Kingsley

Chester's Way by Kevin Henkes

Dad and Me in the Morning by Patricia Lakin

The Day the Crayons Came Home by Drew Daywalt

Each Kindness by Jacqueline Woodson

Emmanuel's Dream: The True Story of Emmanuel Ofosu Yeboah by Laurie Ann Thompson

Enemy Pie by Derek Munson

The Family Book by Todd Parr

Fly Away Home by Eve Bunting

Freedom Summer by Deborah Wiles

Goin' Someplace Special by Patricia C. McKissack

Henry's Freedom Box: A True Story from the Underground Railroad by Ellen Levine

Ian's Walk: A Story About Autism by Laurie Lears

In Our Mothers' House by Patricia Polacco

Introducing Teddy by Jessica Walton

The Invisible Boy by Trudy Ludwig

I, Too, Am America by Langston Hughes

Jin Woo by Eve Bunting

King for a Day by Rukhsana Khan

Knock Knock: My Dad's Dream for Me by Daniel Beaty

Lailah's Lunchbox: A Ramadan Story by Reem Faruqi

La La La: A Story of Hope by Kate DiCamillo

Last Stop on Market Street by Matt de la Peña

Mamma Zooms by Jane Cowen-Fletcher

Mango, Abuela, and Me by Meg Medina

Martin's Big Words: The Life of Dr. Martin Luther King, Jr. by Doreen Rappaport

Morris Micklewhite and the Tangerine Dress by Christine Baldacchino

Music for Alice by Allen Say

My Friend Isabelle by Eliza Woloson

My Man Blue by Nikki Grimes

The Mystery at Palace Street School by Sandy Mahony and Mary Lou Brown

The Name Jar by Yangsook Choi

One Green Apple by Eve Bunting

One Love by Cedella Marley

Ron's Big Mission by Rose Blue and Corinne J. Naden

Rosa by Nikki Giovanni

The Sissy Duckling by Harvey Fierstein

The Sneetches and Other Stories by Dr. Seuss

Something Beautiful by Sharon Dennis Wyeth

Stand Tall, Molly Lou Melon by Patty Lovell

Suki's Kimono by Chieri Uegaki

Susan Laughs by Jeanne Willis

A Taste of Colored Water by Matt Faulkner

Those Shoes by Maribeth Boelts

Tight Times by Barbara Shook Hazen

Two Mrs. Gibsons by Toyomi Igus

The Ugly Vegetables by Grace Lin

Visiting Day by Jacqueline Woodson

We're All Wonders by R. J. Palacio

Whistle for Willie by Ezra Jack Keats

White Socks Only by Evelyn Coleman

Whoever You Are by Mem Fox

CHAPTER BOOKS

Amina's Voice by Hena Khan

Counting by 7s by Holly Goldberg Sloan

El Deafo by Cece Bell

Ella Enchanted by Gail Carson Levine

Esperanza Rising by Pam Muñoz Ryan

Fish in a Tree by Lynda Mullaly Hunt

The Hundred Dresses by Eleanor Estes

Inside Out and Back Again by Thanhha Lai

Locomotion by Jacqueline Woodson

Out of My Mind by Sharon M. Draper

Roll of Thunder, Hear My Cry by Mildred D. Taylor

Rules by Cynthia Lord

Stella by Starlight by Sharon M. Draper

The Watsons Go to Birmingham—1963 by Christopher Paul Curtis

Wishtree by Katherine Applegate

Wonder by R. J. Palacio

ONLINE TEACHER RESOURCES

"'Buddy Bench' Creates a Safe Spot for Shy Classmates to Find
  Friends," HuffPost article, www.huffingtonpost.com/entry/
   buddy-bench-students-pittsburgh_us_5655e132e4b079b28189dcd2

CHAPTER 8

Lending a Helping Hand

When I was a boy and I would see scary things in the news,
my mother would say to me, "Look for the helpers.
You will always find people who are helping."

—Fred Rogers

Some adults think empathy and the ability to share the perspective of another are beyond a young child. Yet we all have seen toddlers comfort a friend with a hug or a pat. We have witnessed the unsolicited kindness of a preschooler helping another child who is struggling with a button or a zipper. Perhaps we look for too much, for adult-level responses, when what we should notice is basic human kindness.

Young children understand the idea of helping a friend in need. They show care and kindness in surprising ways. As educators we attempt to tap into that natural human tendency to offer a helping hand. Children are taught to be kind and to help one another. When we teach very young children to help others in need, they develop a sense of empathy early and demonstrate civility and "good citizenship" within and beyond the classroom community.

In this chapter we explore ways to lead children to perform acts of kindness, offer a helping hand, and give back. Repeated read-aloud experiences of intentionally selected children's literature and open conversations focused on the theme of helping others extend invitations to think beyond oneself.

Ultimately, the goal is to encourage students to take action to go beyond the text and the four walls of their classroom. In doing so, we believe that children will have a better understanding of themselves, others, and the role we all play as democratic citizens to make a better world. Young children are active agents as they construct understanding of themselves and the world around them. They are aware when injustices occur and therefore have a keen sense of fairness and equity. Using the framework of selection, connection, reflection, action, and next steps, we show how one kindergarten class was inspired to give back to those in need in their local community after reading Katherine Applegate's book *Crenshaw*.

Voices from the Classroom

When Sarah McKinney, kindergarten teacher from Hunt Meadows Elementary in Easley, South Carolina, was introduced to the book *Crenshaw*, she immediately knew that she wanted to share the story with her students. Jackson, the main character in this chapter book, has an imaginary friend named Crenshaw who reappears in his life to help him cope when his family goes through financial hardships and experiences homelessness.

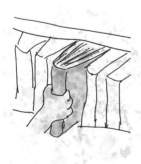

Selection

Crenshaw took on significance for Sarah when a new student joined the class. The child had an unstable home environment and had been bounced around to different homes of various family members. Another student lived with his grandmother because his mom was homeless and unable to provide for him. Sarah knew children whose families struggled due to financial burdens, health issues, and even homelessness. Although Sarah did not share this information with her students, she wanted them to build empathy and understanding for others who may experience hardships in their home lives. Each day she read a chapter from *Crenshaw*, hoping to foster discussion about working-class poverty and homelessness. She and her students examined the circumstances faced by Jackson (the main character) and the challenges he and his family experience as the story unfolds. With his mom's recent layoff from work and his dad's battle with multiple sclerosis, Jackson's family did not have money for rent or much food. They experienced homelessness, which led them to live in their minivan. Interactive read-alouds became a vehicle through which Sarah's kindergartners were able to share their thinking and wondering. Together they examined notions of working-class poverty, resilience, and giving back, all the while developing as compassionate readers.

TAKE A MOMENT TO REFLECT

Sarah thought carefully about the students in her kindergarten class when she made a decision about what book she would read aloud. Think about the students in your class. What book topics or themes might help build empathy and understanding for others? Jot some notes in the margins or in your notebook. ■

Connection

In Chapter 4 of *Crenshaw*, Jackson and his sister play cereal ball to distract themselves from being hungry. They throw Cheerios or little pieces of bread into a bowl or cup and reward themselves by eating it if they score a basket. It was at this pivotal scene in the story that Sarah's students first realized that the characters did not have enough food and were constantly hungry. Later, in Chapter 8, the students learned that Jackson sold his belongings to help pay the bills. The following conversation reveals the connections students made as they attempted to understand Jackson's situation. When asked how they would feel if they were in Jackson's shoes, they responded with feelings of empathy for Jackson as he had to give up his toys and even sell his bed.

> **SARAH:** Now think for a minute. If your mom and dad told you that you had to sell your things, how would you feel?

> STUDENTS: Sad!

STUDENT: One time I had to sell my toy.

STUDENT: Why did they have to sell their things?

SARAH: They have to pay the bills and they have trouble paying the bills. They're even selling the bed.

STUDENT: How are they going to sleep?

STUDENT: If I had to sell my bed, I have a blow-up mattress big enough for my whole family and everyone can fit on it.

SARAH: Remember, they don't have the money to buy new things.

STUDENT: Maybe they can sleep on their couch.

SARAH: I'm not sure if they can keep their couch.

Throughout the day, students continued this conversation. They made connections about selling their toys and donating their toys for other children who may not have as much. One student shared that she was selling some of her toys because her family was moving. These comments and connections demonstrate students' emerging insights and budding empathy for the characters' financial hardship.

CONSIDERATIONS FOR THE **3–6 Classroom**

Crenshaw would be appropriate for students in intermediate grades to read independently, in small groups as part of a book club, or as a read-aloud as Sarah has done with her kindergarten class. This would be a good time to layer in other texts to deepen students' understanding of similar situations. For instance, to extend students' understanding of varying circumstances related to financial hardship, you could read picture books such as *Tight Times* by Barbara Shook Hazen, *Fly Away Home* by Eve Bunting, *Maddi's Fridge* by Lois Brandt, *A Shelter in Our Car* by Monica Gunning,

Still a Family: A Story About Homelessness by Brenda Reeves Sturgis, *Uncle Willie and the Soup Kitchen* by DyAnne DiSalvo-Ryan, and *Last Stop on Market Street* by Matt de la Peña. To extend students' developing knowledge of economic diversity, we recommend reading a variety of books that take place around the world. For instance, *Biblioburro* by Jeanette Winter takes place in Colombia, *Ada's Violin* by Susan Hood takes place in Paraguay, and *Beatrice's Goat* by Page McBrier takes place in Uganda. ▪

Reflection

The previous conversation demonstrates how Sarah's students experienced some tensions as they constructed their understanding of the hardships faced by Jackson's family. Specifically, when they learned that the family had to sell Jackson's bed, they were confused and wondered where the family would sleep. They were committed to helping Jackson's family solve their problem and offered suggestions for alternative sleeping arrangements such as buying an air mattress or sleeping on the couch. Although well intended, these notions reflect the young children's lack of understanding of the family's financial situation and the root causes of their instability. Yet their limited understanding did not prevent them from wanting to take action to help Jackson's family. These kindergartners had strong convictions about helping others: when a student proclaimed, "We need to help Jackson's family!" others responded with a chorus of "Yeah!" and "Let's help Jackson!" Sarah explained that Jackson was a fictional character but children and families in their community and around the world experience hardships like those faced by Jackson's family.

Upon hearing this, the students instantly wanted to know what they could do to help other boys and girls like Jackson. Together they brainstormed ideas such as collecting and sending money, writing letters with money in the envelope, and donating their toys, food, and books.

FOR YOUR CLASSROOM
Share Stories About What Other Children Are Doing to Help

It might be helpful to share other examples of ways that even young children are helping those in need. For instance, the book *The Mitten Tree* by Candace Christiansen could be paired with the video that shares the story of fifth graders in Massachusetts who knit scarves and hats for the homeless (http://wwlp. com/2017/11/15/5th-graders-knit-scarves-and-hats-for-the-homeless/).

Students can also read an article to learn about ten-year-old Jonas Corona, who began a nonprofit to help homeless people in his community (www.huffingtonpost.com/2014/02/06/love-in-the-mirror-nonprofit-homeless_n_4737945.html).

The *Chocolate Bar* book was written and published by six-year-old Dylan Siegel to raise money for a cure for his friend's rare liver condition. Students can visit the website (http://chocolatebarbook.com/) to learn more about the project.

It may also be helpful to have a representative from a service agency come in to share how others in the community help when people are in need.

After doing some research, Sarah learned about the Dream Center, a community center that provides support and resources to individuals and families in need; 37 percent of the walk-ins are homeless. Sarah found out that the center needed hygiene items. She told her students about the Dream Center and they decided they would collect hygiene items to donate. In a follow-up conversation, Sarah helped her students see how they could lend a helping hand and also create a larger movement by informing others of their cause.

> **SARAH:** Do you guys remember we are going to be collecting soap and what else?

> **STUDENT:** Shampoo!

> **STUDENT:** Toothbrushes and toothpaste.

> **STUDENT:** What if they don't have any money?

> **SARAH:** Well, then they would go to the pantry. The pantry gives them the items they need. So at the Dream Center, the place we are helping, people can go get food, clothes, and the soaps and shampoos that we are going to collect.

Once the students decided their plan was to give back to their community by collecting and donating items to the Dream Center, it was time to put their plan into action.

Action

With Sarah's guidance, the kindergartners set a goal to collect one hundred toiletry items by the one hundredth day of school to donate to the Dream Center. They shared information about their project with the school and the community using signs and a digital flyer posted on the class blog and on social media (https://www.smore.com/x0d3n-100-hygiene-items-by-the-100th-day). Figure 8–1 shows a photo of a student holding a sign. Figure 8–2 (https://bit.ly/2G6RcVF) shows the digital flyer the class created and shared on Twitter.

FIGURE 8–1 (above) Kindergarten Student Holds Up a Sign About the Class Project

FIGURE 8–2 (right) Digital Flyer Shared on Twitter

FIGURE 8–3 Students Sort Items into Groups

Sarah developed related math lessons in which students classified the donated items into groups. Then they worked together to count the total number of items in each group. Figure 8–3 shows the class in action as they sort.

All grade levels became involved, and in just one week the digital flyer had over 300 visitors and the class had collected over 50 items. The following week they had a total of 256 items donated, surpassing their goal of 100. Figure 8–4 shows one of the bins they used. By the second week, they reached a grand total of 350 items, as noted by the teacher's updates on social media in Figure 8–5.

They received feedback including the following reply: "Creating an awareness of needs around them is such an important component for the students as they gather these items. Well done, Mrs. McKinney" (Facebook post, January 13, 2016).

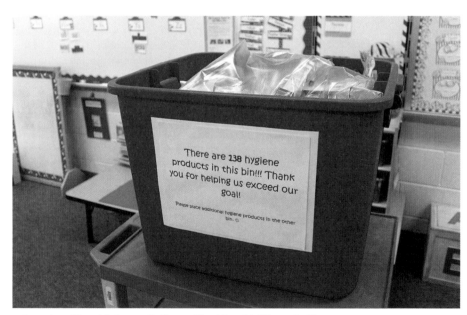

FIGURE 8–4 Bin with Items Collected by Mrs. McKinney's Class

As the drive was a schoolwide effort, the class enthusiastically shared the final total on the school announcements. The following week, a representative from the Dream Center visited Sarah's class to pick up the items, and the students were eager to present their collected goods, as shown in the tweet in Figure 8–6 (https://bit.ly/2UlLzH9). Through this experience, students became change agents and active members of their own community.

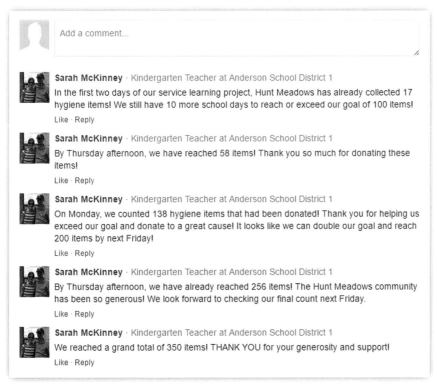

FIGURE 8–5
Teacher Updates on Social Media

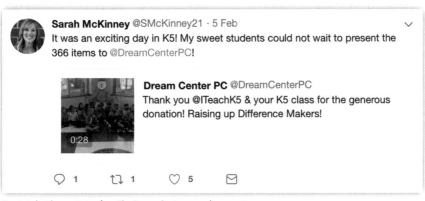

FIGURE 8–6
Sarah's Tweet About the Donations Her Students Helped Collect

Reprinted with permission from The Dream Center, www.dreamcenterpc.org

Next Steps

After reading *Crenshaw* and donating items to the Dream Center, Sarah's students reflected on their lingering thoughts about the book using a combination of drawing and writing. The illustration in Figure 8–7 depicts Jackson's shift from living in the minivan to living in an apartment.

Sarah's lessons about lending a helping hand did not end there. To spark further discussion, she read aloud *A Castle on Viola Street* by DyAnne DiSalvo, *Something Beautiful* by Sharon Dennis Wyeth, and *How to Heal a Broken Wing* by Bob Graham. Students eagerly inquired about other projects. Their compassion and interest in helping was ignited. Sarah encouraged them to find ways to reach out and help their community outside school to extend their learning beyond the classroom and apply their activism in their daily lives.

One day, the school's secretary told Sarah that she saw one of her students over the weekend on the side of the road with his mom and dad not too far from the school. She stopped her car and asked if they were okay. The boy responded that he was just picking up trash. His mom explained that they were driving home and her son insisted they stop because he noticed trash all over the side of the road. He said litter was not good for the people and animals that lived in the community. His parents agreed to

FIGURE 8–7 Student Reflection About *Crenshaw*: "I did not know that they would live in an apartment."

stop and help him pick up the trash. Sarah loved how this little boy saw a problem in his local community and encouraged his parents to help him become part of the solution. The work in school, the collective thinking and action, filtered its way into one child's personal sense of humanity and kindness. That is noteworthy.

Armed with the knowledge that books can cultivate compassionate readers, Sarah purchased and donated a copy of *Crenshaw* to the school's library. The following summer, she applied for a Donors Choose grant to build her classroom library to include more diverse books and to continue to create a community of engaged learners who openly question, analyze, and take action in their world. The grant was fully funded and she purchased thirty-two brand-new books. Her new class of kindergarten students eagerly opened the boxes of books one afternoon and enjoyed scanning book covers and illustrations. The students enjoyed listening to and discussing *Each Kindness* by Jacqueline Woodson, *Dear Primo: A Letter to My Cousin* by Duncan Tonatiuh, *Drum Dream Girl* by Margarita Engle, and *Last Stop on Market Street* by Matt de la Peña, to name a few.

Several of the books, including *Those Shoes* by Maribeth Boelts and *A Shelter in Our Car* by Monica Gunning, sparked an interest in partnering with the Dream Center for a grade-level project. Sarah's class continued the 100 Hygiene Items for the 100th Day project, but this time they were determined to beat the previous year's total. They successfully collected 460 hygiene products! It was exciting for the school's students, families, and staff to partner with the Dream Center for a second year in a row to support their community.

ALTERNATE GRADE EXAMPLE
First Grade

Students in Andrea Phillips' first-grade class at Wyandot Elementary in Dublin, Ohio, learned core values such as kindness and empathy every day as they worked and played together. They used these classroom principles to analyze characters in books they read as a whole class and independently. They tried to understand characters' struggles and made connections to their own lives.

With the emphasis on teaching kindness and empathy as foundational values in Andrea's class, she selected the following collection of texts to read and discuss with her students: *Last Stop on Market Street*, *Those Shoes*, *Fly Away Home*, and *Coat of Many Colors*.

Andrea chose *Coat of Many Colors* by Dolly Parton after she noticed that the main characters in the books read thus far were male and the settings represented predominantly urban areas. Andrea's students immediately noticed the difference in Dolly's mountain home.

> STUDENT: They have so much people in their home.

> STUDENT: Their house is in the grass and ours is on the sidewalk.

> STUDENT: There are no other houses close to it. We have houses next to us.

> STUDENT: They have chickens. It looks like they live on a farm.

Andrea intentionally selected these texts to serve as windows for her students into a variety of dwellings, neighborhoods, and circumstances. She also hoped students would see themselves reflected in the kindness and empathy of the characters.

In *Last Stop on Market Street*, CJ and Nana serve food at the soup kitchen, and in *Those Shoes*, Jeremy gives his sought-after shoes to Antonio. Andrew from *Fly Away Home* demonstrates empathy for the bird that was trapped in the airport. And in *Coat of Many Colors*, as one student explained, "Dolly had empathy for her mom because she worked hard to make the coat. She was proud of her coat." They also noticed that the children at Dolly's school did not have empathy when they laughed at her homemade coat.

During subsequent readings, the students examined the characters' complexities. They noticed that all the main characters wanted something: CJ wanted a car, Jeremy desired shoes, and Andrew wanted a home. But they all already had something even better—love, happiness, family, and friends.

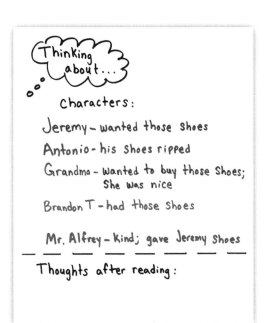

FIGURE 8–8 Character Anchor Chart

And they were all "rich with resilience and persistence." As one student said, "Even if you're poor, you have someone to take care of you." Others chimed in, "They are rich with love." See Figures 8–8 and 8–9 for two character anchor charts the class created.

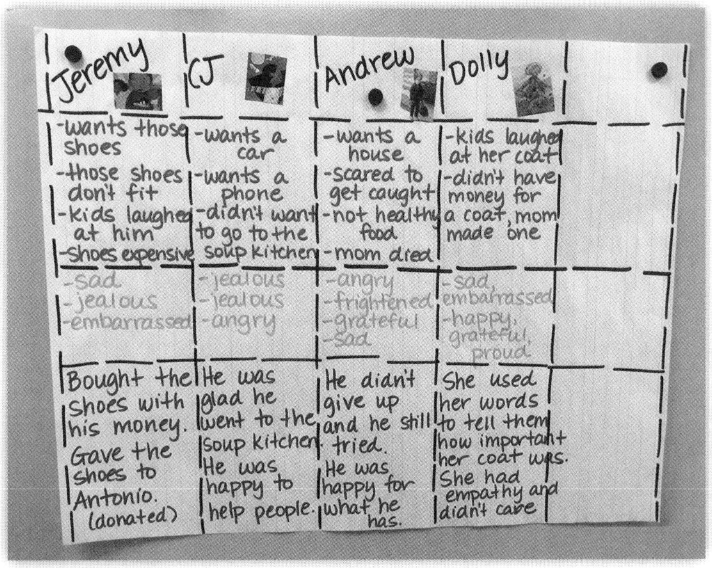

FIGURE 8–9 Anchor Chart Comparing Characters

FOR YOUR CLASSROOM
Lesson on Character Traits

Notice how Andrea starts by talking about and charting basic character traits, as shown in the anchor chart in Figure 8–8. Then, as the chart in Figure 8–9 illustrates, she asks students to examine them more carefully by listing

- what we know about the character,
- how the character might feel, and
- what evidence we have from the text.

Consider creating a similar series of anchor charts by moving students from basic character traits to a more complex examination, citing evidence from the text.

To help move students toward action, Andrea read the book *Ordinary Mary's Extraordinary Deed* by Emily Pearson. In the story, Mary picks blueberries for her neighbor and ignites a kindness chain that spreads around the world. Just like Mary, Andrea's students decided that they too could change the world with their actions.

In Figure 8–10 you can see the "World Changing List" her class created. They marked the actions they could take today. Figures 8–11 and 8–12 show photos of students making "Change the World" posters to hang in their school. The insights and actions of these young children prove the power of literature to move readers. It is clear from the story of their class that even our youngest students are changed by the experience of living through stories.

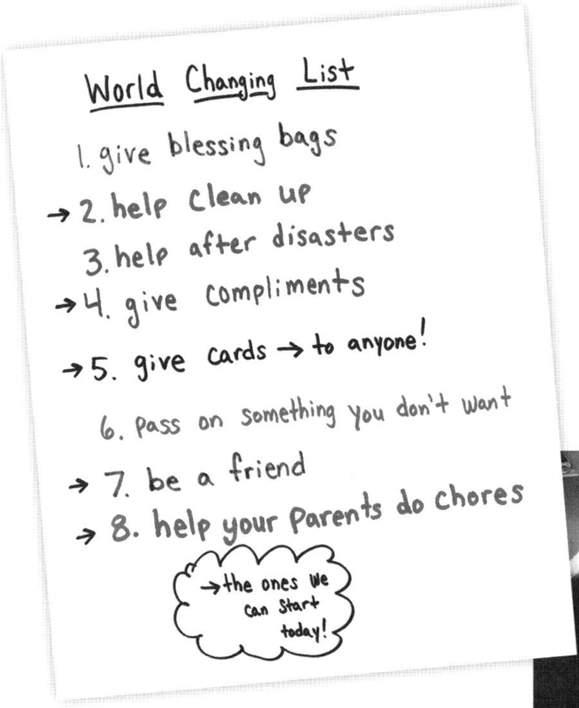

World Changing List
1. give blessing bags
→ 2. help clean up
3. help after disasters
→ 4. give compliments
→ 5. give cards → to anyone!
6. pass on something you don't want
→ 7. be a friend
→ 8. help your parents do chores
→ the ones we can start today!

FIGURE 8–10 (left)
"World Changing List" Anchor Chart

FIGURE 8–11 (center)
One Student Works on His "Change the World" Poster

FIGURE 8–12 (bottom)
Students Show the "Change the World" Posters They Made to Hang Around the School

temperature
1. Help people
2. Clean up
3. Give people 128,000,000 ice creams
4. Give cards
Give candy
Give love

help clean up
2. help after disasters
3. give complimtents
4. give cards (any time)
5. be a friend
the ones we can do every day
Team 18

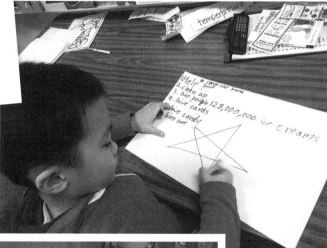

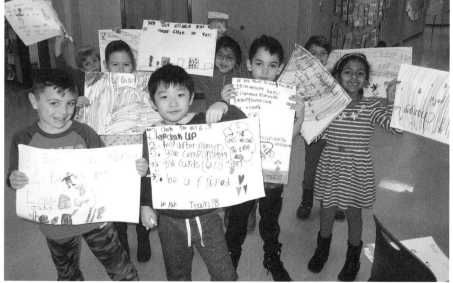

ALTERNATE GRADE EXAMPLE
Third Grade

Roslyn Clapp and her third-grade students at Francine Delany New School for Children in Asheville, North Carolina, chose to take a close look at three books focused on making your world a more beautiful place. Roslyn chose *Miss Rumphius* by Barbara Cooney, *Maybe Something Beautiful: How Art Transformed a Neighborhood* by F. Isabel Campoy and Theresa Howell, and *Something Beautiful* by Sharon Dennis Wyeth. Together they examined the main characters and the challenges they faced. They carefully analyzed the characters and collectively observed a recurring theme across books: finding beauty in your own life leads to sharing beauty with others.

Roslyn began with *Miss Rumphius* and explored the notion that we each have a responsibility to make the world more beautiful. This message is a window to many students who believe they are too young, not yet powerful enough, and not able to make a difference. This book demonstrates how small acts can have a lasting impact.

ROSLYN: How can you use this story in your own life? What themes arise during the story?

STUDENT: Grandfather tells Alice to do something to make the world more beautiful.

STUDENT: Yeah, and Alice grows up and when she is old she tells her great-niece Alice to make the world more beautiful. Hey, they are both named Alice.

STUDENT: I wonder if this message is being passed along throughout the family.

ROSLYN: Oh, so you think maybe the grandfather's grandfather told him to make the world more beautiful. And now he is passing that idea along to his granddaughter, Alice. And then Alice passes it along to her great-niece. Interesting.

Roslyn scaffolded their thinking while allowing them to arrive at insights in their own time.

> STUDENT: I think it's not about making the world prettier; it's about making it more beautiful. It could be like stopping or solving a problem.

> **ROSLYN:** So there are many ways to make the world more beautiful?

> STUDENT: One way that people make our world more beautiful is by fighting for their rights and fighting for other people's rights.

> STUDENT: It doesn't have to be visual–it can just be standing up for yourself and your rights.

> **ROSLYN:** Why would the grandfather tell Alice to make the world a more beautiful place?

> STUDENT: The world is never the most beautiful it can be and there's always something more that you can do to help–the world is never perfect.

Roslyn's students focused their attention on Miss Rumphius' decision to make the world more beautiful and how that was inspiring them to think about what they could do in their own lives.

Roslyn wanted her students to see how a little girl, perhaps near their age, could use her talents to inspire others and make their community a more beautiful place. She read *Maybe Something Beautiful* as a movie read (Laminack 2016)—a reading from start to finish with no stops to turn and talk or ask questions—and reminded the students to enjoy the story, to connect where their minds take them and where their hearts take them, and then to reflect for a while. A few days later, she read the book again and invited the students to think about how this little girl made a difference in her community. Reflecting on the actions of a young girl served as yet another window for Roslyn's students as they considered how a child can lead a community.

ROSLYN: Let's reflect a moment and think about the "so what?" Why does this book matter for us?

STUDENT: If we had never read this book, we would never think of how we could do things in our life.

STUDENTS IN UNISON: Yeah, yes.

ROSLYN: What do you guys think about that idea?

STUDENT: Everyone can help. It can't just be by yourself. Everyone can make a change to the world.

Roslyn listened as her students made connections to the simple things young people can do to make their community a more beautiful place. Then she nudged them to move toward thinking about actions they could take. Notice how she doesn't tell them what to do; they come up with their own ideas.

ROSLYN: Us too? Really? Can we make a change? Talk to me more about that idea. Us, us third graders, this class today, what could we do that would make a change in the world?

STUDENT: If you see some dead flowers, then you could go replace dead flowers with new ones. If you see something sad and you feel like you can help it, then go help it.

STUDENT: Cleaning up garbage and recycling.

STUDENT: Yeah, no littering. And we could build more composting.

STUDENT: If you see, like, homeless people, you could help them out. You could give them blankets or food.

STUDENT: If you see somebody sad, you can try to cheer them up.

STUDENT: You could plant things to make the world more beautiful.

Slowly Roslyn led her students toward a more local, more personal understanding of the power they have to help make the world a more beautiful place. Roslyn and her students had more conversations about *Maybe Something Beautiful*. Then she read aloud *Something Beautiful*. Roslyn invited her class to think about ways these two books and *Miss Rumphius* connect and could lead them toward taking action in the community around their school.

ROSLYN: Let's think about the three books we have studied. Take a look at our chart [see Figures 8-13a and 8-13b] and let's think about what we've noticed.

STUDENT: *Something Beautiful, Maybe Something Beautiful,* and *Miss Rumphius* were connected because they all took place in a town or a neighborhood. I think there were a few places where people weren't treated kindly, but at the end things turned out well.

STUDENT: All the stories started out really gray and negative, but then they found an idea to change the world, and they did it.

ROSLYN: Could we modify that part, "and they did it," to say, "and they took action"?

[Students nod in agreement.]

STUDENT: Unlike in *Miss Rumphius,* they're taking something away. In both *Maybe Something Beautiful* and *Something Beautiful,* they're taking the bad things away and adding new stuff to make beauty. So I think that's how they're similar.

As the students zoomed in on a single title, Roslyn continued to pull back the lens and nudged them to notice the theme cutting across the collection.

Title	Character	Plot	What changes? How is the problem solved? Outcome?
Miss Rumphius	· Ms. Rumphius · Grandpa	Grandpa tells her to make the world more beautiful. She travels to far away places. She lives by the sea. She spreads Lupins and tells her great niece Alice to make the world more beautiful.	The thing that changes is Miss Rumphius because she found her thing (how to make the world more beautiful.) Outcome = The world is more beautiful
Maybe Something Beautiful	· Mira · The Muralist	Her town was gray. Mira hands out paintings. She bumps into the Muralist. Together they paint the walls with bright colors. People join in the paint party. It turns out that the whole town becomes more beautiful.	What changes is the town isn't droopy and gray. It is colorful, exciting, and happy. Everyone is happy. Everyone feels more valued in their placement (neighborhood). People were able to change their own neighborhood.
Something Beautiful	· The Little girl	The girl sees her neighborhood with trash and broken glass. She goes around her neighborhood asking people about their Something beautiful. She learns about other people's something beautiful. She cleans up her courtyard and feels powerful. In the end, the girl is her mother's something beautiful.	She didn't know what her something beautiful was. She took control and felt powerful when she erased the word 'DIE.'

FIGURES 8–13a and 8–13b
Anchor Chart Comparing Texts

How is the plot similar or different from other books we've read?	Theme Message	So What? Why does it matter?
They both changed a small space.	Make the world more beautiful.	You can change the world at any time. There is no limit to making the world more beautiful
Both books change the world and make it more beautiful. Both are small acts that make a big difference.	Color brings out people. It brightens things up. You can get help to make one small part of the world better.	If we had never read this book, then we would never think we could also make a difference.
All the stories start out gray and negative. Then they find a way to change the world and take action. Each character has to find their own thing to make the world better.	Never stop thinking you can find your own thing to make the world more beautiful.	People will be happy. We are the people who change things to be good. Dominos. If we all decide one little part, it spreads. We don't want to live in a bad place.

> **ROSLYN:** The character follows what is in her heart and finds somebody else who has that. In all the stories, each character has to find their own thing. What do you think the message from these three books would be?

> **STUDENT:** You can change the world at any time.

> **STUDENT:** They all had something to do with making the world more colorful.

> **STUDENT:** Maybe the theme or message is to never stop thinking you can make something beautiful.

Students continued to reflect. Roslyn gently led them back toward using these new insights to take some action, to make a difference in their own community.

> **ROSLYN:** Never stop thinking you can find your own thing to make the world more beautiful. Because the characters found their own thing. Why does this matter?

> **STUDENT:** You can make the world more beautiful and it will make people happy.

> **STUDENT:** It's kind of like dominoes. If one person does their part and another person does their part and eventually everyone helps a little bit, then everything will be pretty nice. A little bit goes a long way. Eventually it'll add up to the whole world being nice, because if we all do one little part, then . . . it spreads.

These third graders decided to follow the examples set by the characters they had studied and launched a campaign to bring beauty and joy into the community surrounding their school. Figure 8–14 shows students on the sidewalks to make a more beautiful community.

FIGURE 8–14 **Students Walking in the Local Community with Signs and Flowers**

Suggested Resources

PICTURE BOOKS

Ada's Violin: The Story of the Recycled Orchestra of Paraguay by Susan Hood

Beatrice's Goat by Page McBrier

Biblioburro: A True Story from Colombia by Jeanette Winter

A Castle on Viola Street by DyAnne DiSalvo

A Chair for My Mother by Vera B. Williams

Chicken Sunday by Patricia Polacco

Coat of Many Colors by Dolly Parton

Dear Primo: A Letter to My Cousin by Duncan Tonatiuh

Drum Dream Girl by Margarita Engle

Each Kindness by Jacqueline Woodson

Fly Away Home by Eve Bunting

Frog and Toad All Year by Arnold Lobel

The Great Kapok Tree by Lynne Cherry

How to Heal a Broken Wing by Bob Graham

Last Stop on Market Street by Matt de la Peña

Maddi's Fridge by Lois Brandt

Mama, I'll Give You the World by Roni Schotter

Maybe Something Beautiful: How Art Transformed a Neighborhood by F. Isabel Campoy and Theresa Howell

Miss Rumphius by Barbara Cooney

The Mitten Tree by Candace Christiansen

My Friend Is Sad (an Elephant and Piggie book) by Mo Willems

Ordinary Mary's Extraordinary Deed by Emily Pearson

Rechenka's Eggs by Patricia Polacco

Seeds of Change by Jen Cullerton Johnson

A Shelter in Our Car by Monica Gunning

A Sick Day for Amos McGee by Philip C. Stead

Something Beautiful by Sharon Dennis Wyeth

Still a Family: A Story About Homelessness by Brenda Reeves Sturgis

Those Shoes by Maribeth Boelts

Tight Times by Barbara Shook Hazen

The Trees of the Dancing Goats by Patricia Polacco

Uncle Willie and the Soup Kitchen by DyAnne DiSalvo-Ryan

Wangari's Trees of Peace: A True Story from Africa by Jeanette Winter

Wilfrid Gordon McDonald Partridge by Mem Fox

CHAPTER BOOKS

Alia's Mission: Saving the Books of Iraq by Mark Alan Stamaty

Because of Winn-Dixie by Kate DiCamillo

The Boy Who Harnessed the Wind by William Kamkwamba and Bryan Mealer

Crenshaw by Katherine Applegate

Fish in a Tree by Lynda Mullaly Hunt

Ghost by Jason Reynolds

A Long Walk to Water by Linda Sue Park

The One and Only Ivan by Katherine Applegate

Rules by Cynthia Lord

Seedfolks by Paul Fleischman

A Single Shard by Linda Sue Park

Where the Mountain Meets the Moon by Grace Lin

Wishtree by Katherine Applegate

REFERENCES

Adichie, Chimamanda Ngozi. 2009. "The Danger of a Single Story." TED video. www.ted.com/talks/chimamanda_adichie_the_danger_of_a_single_story.

Au, Kathryn. 1980. "Participation Structures in a Reading Lesson with Hawaiian Children: Analysis of a Culturally Appropriate Instructional Event." *Anthropology & Education Quarterly* 11 (2): 91–115.

Bishop, Rudine Sims. 1990. "Multicultural Literacy: Mirrors, Windows, and Sliding Glass Doors." *Perspectives: Choosing and Using Books for the Classroom* 6 (3). https://scenicregional.org/wp-content/uploads/2017/08/Mirrors-Windows-and -Sliding-Glass-Doors.pdf.

Boelts, Maribeth. 2007. *Those Shoes.* Somerville, MA: Candlewick Press.

Bomer, Randy, and Katherine Bomer. 2001. *For a Better World: Reading and Writing for Social Action.* Portsmouth, NH: Heinemann

Botelho, Maria José, and Masha Kabakow Rudman. 2009. *Critical Multicultural Analysis of Children's Literature: Mirrors, Windows, and Doors.* Language, Culture, and Teaching series. New York: Routledge.

Boutte, Gloria Swindler. 2008. "Beyond the Illusion of Diversity: How Early Childhood Teachers Can Promote Social Justice." *Social Studies* 99 (4): 165–73.

Boyd, Fenice B., Lauren L. Causey, and Lee Galda. 2015. "Culturally Diverse Literature: Enriching Variety in an Era of Common Core State Standards." *Reading Teacher* 68 (5): 378–87.

Christ, Tanya, and Sue Ann Sharma. 2018. "Searching for Mirrors: Preservice Teachers' Journey Toward More Culturally Relevant Pedagogy." *Reading Horizons* 57 (1): 55–73.

Davis, Angela. 2016. "Nicholtown Determined to Rise from Tragedy." *Greenville News,* March 25. www.greenvilleonline.com/story/news/2016/03/25/nicholtown -determined-rise-tragedy/82159278/.

de la Peña, Matt. 2018. "Why We Shouldn't Shield Children from Darkness." *Time,* January 9, 2018. http://time.com/5093669/why-we-shouldnt-shield-children -from-darkness/.

DiCamillo, Kate. 2018. "Why Children's Books Should Be a Little Sad." *Time,* January 12, 2018. http://time.com/5099463/kate-dicamillo-kids-books-sad/.

Ebe, Ann E. 2010. "Culturally Relevant Texts and Reading Assessment for English Language Learners." *Reading Horizons* 50 (3): 193–210.

Gambrell, Linda B. 2011. "Seven Rules of Engagement: What's Most Important to Know About Motivation to Read." *Reading Teacher* 65 (3): 172–78.

Garth-McCullough, Ruanda. 2008. "Untapped Cultural Support: The Influence of Culturally Bound Prior Knowledge on Comprehension Performance." *Reading Horizons* 49 (1): 1–30.

Ghani, Amarra. 2018. "On This Bench, You May Find a Buddy; PLP Student Inspired by *Wonder* Book." *Mooresville Citizen*, March 15, 2018. www.lakenormanpublications.com/mooresville_citizen/on-this-bench-you-may-find-a-buddy-plp-student/article_258d1d68-287e-11e8-9c74-8b513ec42c5d.html.

Grimes, Nikki. 2016. Luncheon Presentation at South Carolina Chapter of the International Reading Association (SCIRA) Conference.

Guthrie, John T., and Allan Wigfield. 2000. "Engagement and Motivation in Reading." In *Handbook of Reading Research*, vol. 3, edited by Michael L. Kamil, Peter B. Mosenthal, P. David Pearson, and Rebecca Barr, 403–22. Mahwah, NJ: Erlbaum.

Guthrie, John T., Allan Wigfield, and Wei You. 2012. "Instructional Contexts for Engagement and Achievement in Reading." In *Handbook of Research on Student Engagement*, edited by Sandra L. Christenson, Amy L. Reschly, and Cathy Wylie, 601–34. New York: Springer.

hooks, bell. 2004. *Skin Again.* New York: Jump at the Sun.

Keene, Ellin Oliver, and Susan Zimmermann. 2007. *Mosaic of Thought: The Power of Comprehension Strategy Instruction*. 2nd ed. Portsmouth, NH: Heinemann.

Kurkjian, Catherine, and Nancy Livingston. 2007. "The Importance of Children's Literature in a Global Society." *Reading Teacher* 60 (6): 594–602.

Laminack, Lester L. 2016. *The Ultimate Read-Aloud Resource: Making Every Moment Intentional and Instructional with Best Friend Books.* New York: Scholastic.

Levis, Caron. 2016. *Ida, Always*. New York: Atheneum.

Mankiw, Sue, and Janis Strasser. 2013. "Tender Topics: Exploring Sensitive Issues with Pre-K Through First Grade Children Through Read-Alouds." *Young Children* 68 (1): 84–89.

Mobin-Uddin, Asma. 2005. *My Name Is Bilal*. Honesdale, PA: Boyds Mills Press.

Moll, Luis C., Cathy Amanti, Deborah Neff, and Norma Gonzalez. 1992. "Funds of Knowledge for Teaching: Using a Qualitative Approach to Connect Homes and Classrooms." *Theory into Practice* 31 (2): 132–41.

Morgan, Hani, and Kathleen C. York. 2009. "Examining Multiple Perspectives with Creative Think-Alouds." *Reading Teacher* 63 (4): 307–11.

Myers, Walter Dean. 2014. "Where Are the People of Color in Children's Books?" *New York Times*, March 15, 2014. www.nytimes.com/2014/03/16/opinion /sunday/where-are-the-people-of-color-in-childrens-books.html.

Pennell, Ashley E., Barbara Wollak, and David A. Koppenhaver. 2017. "Respectful Representations of Disability in Picture Books." *Reading Teacher* 71 (4): 411–19.

Rosenblatt, Louise M. 1995. *Literature as Exploration.* 5th ed. New York: Modern Language Association.

Say, Allen. 2004. *Music for Alice.* New York: Houghton Mifflin.

Sharma, Sue Ann, and Tanya Christ. 2017. "Five Steps Toward Successful Culturally Relevant Text Selection and Integration." *Reading Teacher* 71 (3): 295–307.

Shire, Warsan. n.d. "Home." Accessed September 22, 2018. https://genius.com /Warsan-shire-home-annotated.

Sims, Rudine. 1983. "Strong Black Girls: A 10-Year-Old Responds to Fiction About Af-ro-Americans." *Journal of Research and Development in Education* 16 (3): 21–28.

Souto-Manning, Mariana, Carmen Lugo Llerena, Jessica Martell, Abigail Salas Maguire, and Alicia Arce-Boardman. 2018. *No More Culturally Irrelevant Teaching.* Portsmouth, NH: Heinemann.

Souto-Manning, Mariana, and Jessica Martell. 2016. *Reading, Writing, and Talk: Inclusive Teaching Strategies for Diverse Learners, K–2.* New York: Teachers College Press.

St. Amour, Melissa J. 2003. "Connecting Children's Stories to Children's Literature: Meeting Diversity Needs." *Early Childhood Education Journal* 31 (1): 47–51.

Stover, Katie, and Lindsay Yearta. 2017. *From Pencils to Podcasts: Digital Tools for Transforming K–6 Literacy Practices.* Bloomington, IN: Solution Tree.

Tarshis, Lauren. 2015. "The Day Mrs. Parks Was Arrested." *Scholastic Storyworks* 22 (4): 14–19.

Tatum, Alfred W. 2000. "Breaking Down Barriers That Disenfranchise African American Adolescent Readers in Low-Level Tracks." *Journal of Adolescent and Adult Literacy* 44 (1): 52–64.

———. 2006. "Engaging African American Males in Reading." *Educational Leadership* 63 (5): 44–49. http://www.ascd.org/ASCD/pdf/journals/ed_lead /el200602_tatum.pdf.

Tatum, Alfred W., and Gholnecsar E. Muhammad. 2012. "African American Males and Literacy Development in Contexts That Are Characteristically Urban." *Urban Education* 47 (2): 434–63.

Teaching Tolerance. n.d. "Discovering My Identity." Accessed September 25, 2018. www.tolerance.org/classroom-resources/tolerance-lessons/discovering -my-identity.

Vasquez, Vivian, and Carol Felderman. 2012. *Technology and Critical Literacy in Early Childhood*. New York: Routledge.

Vygotsky, Lev S. 1978. *Mind in Society: The Development of Higher Psychological Processes*. Cambridge, MA: Harvard University Press.

ADDITIONAL RESOURCES TO ENHANCE YOUR READING AND WRITING INSTRUCTION FROM
LESTER L. LAMINACK

For more from Lester L. Laminack, including professional development opportunities, visit **hein.pub/LesterLaminack**